What Sisters Are Saying About the Poems In
A Book of Poetry A Sister Can Eat To

This poetry stays rooted in you because it plants such a deep seed. See, it's easy to believe in the things that we can see because they are right in front of us. However, our challenge is belief in the things that we cannot see. That's why the scripture says that we walk by faith and not by sight. This is a different form of praise and worship. These poems reflect some situations that would wipe the average person out but prove that if you have the courage to stand and not run and hold onto your faith, you will come out victorious! And so will others!

Evangelist Chellette Thaxton
Prophecyoriginal

These poems express life and the word of God is the only thing that will deliver us from strongholds and this book of poems will set us free (John 8:36). And the recipes not only remind me but other sisters about the importance of the simple things in life like cooking.

Prophetess Karen Wright
Jesus Cares

Meochia taps into the heart and mind of women in such a mind-boggling way. Her honesty and willingness to share from the heart place you right where she was/is. These poems leave you wanting to read, learn, and grow more.

Evangelist Shelli Dew
Ministerial Alliance/Sisterhood Connection

To Kiss A King
To me as a wife and a woman that is in love with God, it stirs up the love that is on the inside of me for God and my Husband and makes me want to spread love even more, and use these recipes to light the fire!

First Lady, Vonnie Matthews
Extraordinary Women Doing Extraordinary Things

The Best Thing
I think that many women can relate to it...the allure and captivism of sin and sensuality. Deep down as women, we know what we want but we allow the trappings of the flesh to convince us to follow lies. It brings a constant reminder to us that if in the end we aren't standing firm in God's standard, being honest with Him, ourselves, and others, that we'll fall into the trap over again.

Angel Files
Chosen Through Trauma

From Black Son To Mother

This poem is confirming to me personally that I have done a wonderful job with my son. I guided to a point that he needed me near and then I was able to let go with confidence that he would soar. To a mom holding on to her son, it inspires her to give him the wings needed to fly away, knowing that his course will lead him back if needed. The message is clearly stated. The prayer is brief and rightly so. The poem expressed a great deal of feeling. God doesn't need details on what he already knows. The recipe is really nice and tasty. I enjoyed it with grits. It is good for this poem because it represents just how to keep an eye out but not smother your son.

Deborah Anderson
G.R.A.C.E.
Board of Ushers, ACOG

Pruned to Bloom

Pruning is necessary for flowers to grow into their full beauty and potential. As women, we can be wounded but with God's restoration, we can become the true beauties we were meant to be, inside and out. Women are fragile but also uniquely strong at the same time. We can be damaged but can re-blossom!

Faye Tippy
Apostolic Church of God

A
Book of Poetry
A Sister Can Eat To
Nourishment for the Mind, Body, and Soul

Meochia Nochi Thompson

Meochia Nochi Blount Publishing

Blessed Pen Ink / Blessed Pen, Inc.

Blessed Pen Ink
P.O. Box 386
Flossmoor, IL 60422

Join us at meochianochi.com

Printed in the United States of America

Blessed Pen Ink is a division of Meochia Nochi Blount Publishing

Scripture taken from the HOLY BIBLE, NEW INTERNATIONAL VERSION ®. Copyright © 1973, 1978, 1984 by International Bible Society. Used by permission of Zondervan. All rights reserved.

Library of Congress Control Number: 2011911138

ISBN-10 0-9740777-0-4
ISBN-13 978-0-9740777-0-3

Cover Illustration by Keisha Jordan.

This book is dedicated to my daughter, Disha Roddy, one of the most beautiful and wise little sisters I know. And to one of the best cooks in the world, my mother, Shannon Sanders, who taught me that faith and confidence open the doors to the world and unlock unlimited opportunities. Also, all my sisters who may have lost their way, or are searching for the right path, or just need confirmation. God bless you and all of your precious gifts!

ಏಬಏಬಏ

Dear Lord, when I was in the world, thinking of coming to you seemed to be a punishment but I must confess to all that can hear and see that it has truly been a privilege.

Table of Contents

Acknowledgements

First and foremost, I would like to thank God for giving me the gift of words and staying true to His promises. I am so lost without You, Lord and I am glad I finally surrendered to You. Some may argue that the Lord does not speak to His people anymore but I know for a fact that He does. I pray to continue to walk in faith and always be obedient to Your voice because You never steer me wrong, even when things seem grim, You are faithful. I will thank and praise You all the days of my life! It took 10 years to complete this book but I know You were waiting on my faith and wisdom to catch up with the gifts You gave me. I love You, Lord.

I would also like to thank my oldest daughter, Disha Khadija Roddy, for being my most supportive fan base! It melted my heart when you looked at me after this book was complete and said, "Momma, I am so proud of you!" You were my first true investor and I love you so much for putting that much faith in my gift!

My mom, Shannon Lee Sanders, for being very understanding about the personal experiences I share in this book and trusting that it would encourage and inspire others who are on their way through, are going through or have been through similar issues.

My precious son, who is also my little chef's assistant and taste tester, Broc A. Thompson. He loved every recipe and even gave me a few tips to make my cooking even better.

My "superman" of a husband, Minister Curtis A. Thompson, thank you for recognizing my gifts from our first date and helping me get an audience with God's people and for sharing your life with me.

I would also like to acknowledge the 14 women of God, who took the time out of their busy schedules to help revise and review each poem, recipe, testimony, scripture, and prayer to make sure they were biblically sound and on point. I love each of you because you have touched my life significantly; First Ladies (Lennaire Vaughn and Vonnie Matthews); Evangelists (Zaleeta Walker, Karen Wright, Doris Davenport, Chellette Thaxton, Melanie Stagger, Rosalyn Clarke, Tytrea Baker, and Shelli Dew); and

Sisters (Angel Files, Faye Tippy, Deborah Anderson, and Shellene Rose). Also, hugs and kisses to sister Dolores Durant for all of your pearls of wisdom that you unselfishly spilled upon me.

All of my siblings and my entire family for encouraging me with my writings and recipes throughout my life but especially my big brother, Andrew Blount, who has to be the most thorough researcher I know. You stayed on top of me and helped me become a finisher!

My brilliant cousin, Sharlyne Thomas, who has a way with words and knows how to get a job done and Daeshaunn DeLong Brown, my last minute emergency kit.

My "other" best friend, Dave Watkins, who kept me focused on the promises of God for me as a wife, woman, and mother. And to his lovely wife, Michelle, who cut out an awesome pattern of what determination, patience, and sacrifice looks like for a wife following the will of God!

And last but not least, I would like to acknowledge my beautiful friend, Dove White, who kept encouraging me to hurry up and just get it done already. You are a true treasure.

If I have forgotten anyone, please forgive me and know that even if my flesh has failed to remember, you are still stored in my spirit forever and I thank you, as well!

Foreword

I assume you're hungry because this divine buffet is fit for a queen! Meochia Thompson has redefined the ordinary three-course meal and produced an essential menu to satiate your triune being: poetry and encouragement for the soul, scripture, and prayer for the spirit, and delicious recipes for the body. Even if you're a picky eater, you will undoubtedly find a morsel of wisdom and hope to tickle your palate.

Before this book was completed, I had the pleasure of hearing some of her poems read aloud. They touched my heart so much, especially "Pruned to Bloom," all I could do was cry! Sometimes it's nice to escape into a fictional story that is totally unrelated to you, but how do you feel when an author tells your story without even knowing it? Meochia's writing is more than entertaining, informative, or persuasive — it's almost prophetic because it's real.

From beautiful illustrations of strength to clever injections of humor, you will be inspired by each tasty dish. Meochia's transparency, creativity, and faithfulness along this Spirit-led journey is commendable. She would not have been able to testify of the victory in Jesus if she had not been tested herself. Women (and men) of all ages can learn from her perseverance.

I pray this book will remind you that you are precious in the sight of the Lord and already possess the qualities and resources needed to reach your destiny. Be enlightened and challenged by what you read within these pages, and listen for that still small voice to guide you along your own path to success. Bon appétit!

Sharlyne C. Thomas
Author of *When Heaven Hears Your Prayer*

Introduction

Every woman goes through situations in her life that she is either not prepared for, didn't expect, or needs some non-biased advice on. I have my share of testimony from being a single mom, struggling to put myself through college, baby momma and daddy drama, dating, marriage with a blended family, politics, and wondering what is wrong with half of the people in this world that do the crazy things they do.

My goal is to encourage you to keep going no matter how weird life gets. Not only do I want you to reach for the stars and enjoy all that life has to offer but I also want you to reach for the bible as your guide for answers, comfort, inspiration, and support. Sometimes we have to look beyond our present circumstance and look forward to the future. But in all situations, always remember that Jesus Christ is your source of strength.

These poems aren't "preachy". In fact, a few of them may be considered a little risqué. But, I cannot pretend that as women we don't encompass every emotion from feeling sexy, silly and fun to angry, bitter and mischievous. Like I said before, my goal is to help you push through life's challenges thereby putting you on the road to becoming a 360 Degree Woman, which is a well-rounded, wise woman.

Each poem contains encouraging scriptures, strengthening prayer, and an uplifting explanation. Each explanation provides a comforting meal for you and your loved ones to share. Each meal includes cooking time and serving size. These meals are made for sisters who desire to make the most of their budget, time, and cooking creativity.

It took ten years of stretching, learning, healing, and humbling myself in order for me to listen for and hear God's voice and complete this book. I hope it will be a blessing to you and whomever you decide to share it with.

About the 1st Piece
My Word, My Words

There is power in the tongue. The word of God says that you can speak life or death into existence. Just imagine…the whole world was founded on God's word. It was with Him in the beginning and it is still with us today. We experience it every time we pick up a bible. It remained in our hearts and minds since the first time we learned about the goodness of God. So be careful about the words you choose. Speak words that edify. Speak words of love, peace, happiness, and life. We worship an Almighty God and in the end, his word will be the only thing left standing.

My Word, My Words

Oh but My Word, My Words

Sure as glasses stain and bruises pain
Ears ring at the sound of my name
As definite as summers pass and after rains run dry
And tears drop from sorrowed eyes
Certainly as tomorrows coming and nights fall
As words are written and mothers call

My Word, My Words

How one lie can turn to defy
Make innocent die and mothers cry
One look straight into the eyes
And a for certain glance that won't deny
When truth is released to set free
How it flows between lips so easily
But makes others cringe at having to admit
Their false accusations and unknowing wit

My Word, My Words

How when harshly thrown they sting worse than bees
And when put down firmly stand taller than trees
When promised are worth more karats than gold
Having children waiting until days of old

My Word, My Words

When said softly or spoken in just the right tone
Moistens skin and make bodies moan
If said convincingly, pretty, and quick
Minds get jingled and pockets are picked
When tumbled leaves listeners in disbelief
Pulling uncertainty out of one's grief
When said with force

Calls bodies to attention and eyes to stand still
Shuffling through decisions and closing down on deals
When written are more solid than stone
Making laws and stopping people from being owned
My words are my power and with them I can kill
My heart provides strength
My God is my shield
My words are my army
With each sentence there's a new defense
My knowledge is my justice
My eyes my evidence
When I speak the coldest run chills
Meek follow the truth
I make kings kneel
Bodies grow numb at the sound of my voice
I filter out nonsense and cease all noise
I lead all herds of heard
And guide them with My Word, My Words

Your Words Can Be A Lifesaver or Deathtrap

In my family you were taught the importance of words. So, I knew very early in life that I needed to be careful how I used them.

My mother instilled the bible saying into us about your tongue being like a two-edged sword and how what you say can affect someone's life tremendously, good or bad.

My grandfather always said that your word was your bond. And, my grandmother taught us "nice-nasty". She said you didn't need to shout, curse or fight, but smile and say what you had to say in a normal and decent manner. She said that would hurt someone worse than you getting belligerent and saying something you might end up regretting later. I've learned that no one likes looking like a fool arguing with themselves, either. The bible says to treat your enemies with kindness; your kindness is like heaping coals on their heads. That alone will have more of an affect on them than doing physical harm, any day. Why? It's simple; people look crazy arguing with someone who isn't fussing back, especially to the audience watching.

My grandfather, Mudaddy, had a stroke around 1987. One of the drawbacks was that he was left without the ability to speak. In fact, his vocabulary only consisted of two curse words (one began with a "d" and the other an "s" and he used them quite often and quite well) and "uh-huh" (for yes) and "uh-uh" (for no). When you couldn't figure out what he wanted, he'd just shake his head and laugh at you. We started thinking he was pretending not to speak just so he could shut us up from talking to him. Just think about it for a moment. My grandparents had 12 kids, 96 or more grandkids and 45 great-grandkids, mostly women. He couldn't win if he tried. And our family is still increasing this very day.

Seriously, before Mudaddy (that's what we called him) had his stroke, he had a thunderous voice. When he spoke, everyone would be quiet, immediately. I remember being terrified as a little girl, every time I heard his voice. All he would have to say was hi and I would begin to cry on the spot. His voice alone was powerful. He stood six foot two and was one of the strongest men I have yet to know.

Now, my biological father used his words as a form of trickery. My mom told me that my daddy could make money off selling air. He was a con artist and could speak so fast and quick people wouldn't know what hit them. Although some people did try to kill him because of his sly tactics, others admired him. Mom said some people liked his nerve and gave him more money because of how skilled he was at the art of lying. The sad part is my father got caught up in his own game.

Eventually, my dad's fast talking lifestyle destroyed our family. I think he learned that you can't outsmart, outthink, or outtalk God. Life will catch up with you. But thank God for his loving grace. God offers our poor souls redemption! I hadn't seen my dad in person since I was about 3 years old. However, I made contact with him when I was 15, then we lost touch. I finally found him again when I was 27 years old. Although I opted not to see him, we did speak over the phone and write each other. During that time he also got a chance to build a relationship with my daughter. He even sent me money from time to time. I didn't really need it but I think it made him feel good knowing that he could finally do something for me.

After about two years of going back and forth, I believe he died because after one last phone conversation in 2004, I never heard from him, again. I knew he was still "in the streets" but I wasn't sure to what extent. My poor father became a victim of his own tongue. It seems he went through life not knowing "game" from reality.

I wrote this poem right before my grandfather's death. I wish he could have spoke one more time and told my family to remember our past, our love for each other, and to keep God first.

This poem is about the power of words, the force of voice, and the difference between meaning and noise.

Stretch Chili

3 tablespoons of chili powder
1 packet of chili seasoning mix
2-16 ounce cans of chili beans
16 ounces of spaghetti (optional)
1 stalk of celery (chopped)
½ medium onion (diced small)
½ medium green pepper (diced small)
½ garlic clove (diced small)
1-2 pounds of ground beef or turkey
2-16 ounce cans of tomato sauce
1-16 ounce can of diced tomato
1-8 ounce can of tomato paste

1. In a large pot boil water, then cook spaghetti (optional)
2. Thoroughly cook ground meat in medium frying pan, drain grease
3. Add chili powder and seasoning with water then let simmer
4. Add cans of tomatoes to meat mixture, vegetables, and chili powder
5. Add beans and meat mixture to a large pot. Cover and let simmer for 20 minutes
6. Add spaghetti
7. Cover and let entire mixture simmer for 10 minutes

Servings: 6-8
Prep & Cook time: 1 hour

Suggested Scriptures
John 1:1-5
Proverbs 18:21
Proverbs 16:13-16
James 3:7-12
Matthew 15:17-19
Jeremiah 1:9

Dear Lord,

Bless the words that come from my mouth so that my tongue will not slip but speak deliberate words of healing. Help me to speak words that edify and bring forth encouragement and glorify your name. Lord, forgive me for using my tongue to intentionally kill, wound, and destroy. Bless me with knowledge of your word, help me to build a consistent relationship with you, and give me wisdom to listen to good advice. Thank you for everything. I pray and give thanks in Jesus' name. Amen.

Meochia Nochi Thompson

About the 2nd Piece
I Am Woman

We have to learn to love ourselves for who we are and stop complaining so much about what we are not. As women, we never seem satisfied with how we look. We are either too short or too tall or too big or too small. We need to stop and realize that God made us in his perfect image. It is all about confidence. There is somebody for everyone but if you can't even love yourself fully, flaws and all, who will ever enjoy loving you? You are a helpmeet; a woman of purpose. Your dedication should be to God, your family and yourself. People should look at you and see a reflection of hope, faith, and love. You are beautiful!

I Am Woman

I am Woman
I mean look at me
And not just any kind of woman
I mean real woman

There is no beginning for a woman such as I
And there shall definitely be no ending
I am infinity multiplied by X
Huh, you don't hear me!

See, others look down on me because of my golden
To sumptuous, dark brown complexion
But that don't bother me none though honey

Why? Why don't that bother me?

Because black is beautiful! How the saying go ya'll?
The blacker the berry, the sweeter the juice
And I think it's about time for me to go and get a tan
Huh, you don't hear me!

And what about my largely proportioned lips?
The bigger, the better
So big, in fact, some go and get theirs enlarged just to be like me
But theirs will never be as soft and luscious as mine
Because I am Woman, real Woman
The Black Woman!

And what about my large hips and big behind?
Men of all colors grow short of breath when I walk by
Yes, when I walk by
I hear silent whispers, soft whistles, and coughs

Why? Because I am woman!

I am something to come home to with my soft touch

I am something to look forward to
Because I will always be there
Especially for my man, my black man
We can argue, fuss, and fight
But just like my color is dominant
So is my love, this sweet honey love

Yes, I am fine, I am a sight for the sorest of eyes to see
And my body is so soft, sexy, and curved
It will make the strongest man in the world fall weak...
In my power

My love has a whip appeal
And I am as strong and as hard as steel
I will listen and fight for what is right
Because my grip for my people is tight
I will say what I want, when I want, and how I feel
Because I am woman, black woman, and I am real

You don't hear me. I said I am Real.

The saying goes, "Before me there was none
And after me there shall be no more..."

Because I am Woman, Real Woman, the Black Woman!

The Making of A 360-Degree Woman

I wrote this poem for a fashion and talent show when I was a freshman at Mississippi Valley State in Itta Bena, Mississippi. MVSU is a historically black college. It took me about five minutes to write it but the impact has lasted for as long as I can remember. At first I was afraid to recite the poem because I didn't think my poetry was a competitive or interesting talent to anyone besides my mom and myself. But writing was the only talent that I knew I had back then and trust me, nobody would've wanted to hear me sing. So, I just took a chance, I figured I was blessed and God would not give me a gift to keep me poor or ashamed. So, I just started writing.

My next challenge was figuring out what could hold an audience of my peers attention long enough to hear me out before they'd begin booing me off stage. I knew I needed to write something that appreciated every aspect of a beautiful black woman. She needed to be praised for being a good mother, worker, friend, lover, and wife. I wanted to describe a 360-degree woman. She was going to be beautiful mentally, physically, and spiritually. Soon, the words began forming on paper, I Am Woman. I called home after I wrote it and asked my mother how it sounded. Momma, being my best and worst critic, loved it. After getting her approval, I took a deep breath, memorized it, and dramatized it within three days.

I was all over that stage during the contest; you would have thought it belonged to me! I spoke loud and boldly, held my hands up high, swung my hips, flashed my smile, and walked with confidence. I needed to speak directly to each woman in the audience, so she could feel me and know I felt her. I had on the black dress and high heels; everything I needed to draw my audience in. I couldn't believe I won first place in the talent competition held by the Alphas on campus that night! God showed up, off, and out!

I have to admit the ladies in the audience were uptight at first but when they heard me proudly say, "I am woman, black woman," I won them over! They went wild. It was over. Thank

God for the many gifts he blesses us with. He gives them to us to share with the world not to bury or hide.

I also presented this poem in video format for a production class at Columbia College in Chicago. It was going to serve as a dedication to my Grandmother, Delores, who was diagnosed with lung cancer. It was a wonderful presentation but she never got to be in it because she was too tired. I remember her telling me that she didn't want me to write no poem at her funeral after she was dead. She wanted to hear hers before then. I guess she wanted to decide if she liked it or not.

I went to the hospital where she was and acted out "I Am Woman" for her. My grandmother was so weak she could hardly speak or lift herself up to use the bedpan. But by the time I finished my reading, she smiled and said in a husky, tired voice, "Ooh, you can't touch that baby, I like that." She began to laugh. Next, she slowly got her stubborn behind out of that bed and walked to the bathroom. She came back out and said, "I don't need no bedpan." Then she said that she "wasn't dying in no hospital either" and she wanted to go home. She got her wish, too. She died shortly after that with all twelve of her children and her husband at her bedside, praying together as she passed away. She was one of the strongest, sexiest, funniest, and most beautiful women I knew. I wish she could have told me so much more about her childhood and past. She was the best.

After 12 kids and keeping a man in marriage for 48 years, she knew something that a lot of the sisters of today are missing. Listen, wisdom lies in the cries and eyes of the old. So children should listen when they are talking.

My mother and all of her sisters seemed to cherish womanhood. I believe they got it from my grandmother and great-grandmother. My great-grandmother was 93 before she died and she was still looking good! She laughed, flirted, and always kept herself looking and smelling wonderful. My mother and aunts taught me how to be feminine, confident, smart, and beautiful. They all look great and have their own unique personalities and they are all ladies first. They are all wives. They understand the real strength and power in the meaning of submission.

To be a 360-Degree Woman, you have to be true to yourself. Nobody likes a wannabe or fake. If you don't have the knowledge, seek it because it is important for your daughters, nieces, sisters, and friends. "I Am Woman" is about understanding who you truly are and being the best at it!

Real Deal Squash

2 large potatoes
1 large yellow onion
4 yellow banana squash
1 pound of bacon (optional)
1/3 cup of water
1/4 cup of olive oil
Seasonings: salt, pepper, seasoning salt

1. Fry bacon and cut into one-inch squares or crumble
2. Pour thin layer of oil and leftover bacon grease into large frying pan
3. Cut potatoes, onions, and squash into medium slices
4. Layer each ingredient, including bacon, into pan, and season
5. Pour water into squash mixture
6. Place a cover on frying pan and cook at medium-low temperature
7. Stir ingredients every 10 minutes to avoid sticking

* Meal is complete when potatoes are cooked
* Keep some bacon to the side to layer top for extra crunch

Servings: 4-6
Prep & Cook time: 30-45 minutes

Meochia Nochi Thompson

<u>Suggested Scriptures</u>
Genesis 2:21-23
1 Peter 3:3-6
Proverbs 31:10-31, 18:22
Ephesians 5:2

Dear Lord,

Let my beauty come from the inside out. Let me be a reflection of your goodness and grace, Lord. Help me to guide other women into your marvelous light by my actions and words of righteousness. Oh, keep your hands on me, Lord. Let me be a peacemaker in my home, a model citizen in my community, faithful in my church duties, loving to my husband, and a wonderful example to my children. Lord, cover my head and help me to look to you for guidance when I disagree with my husband. Lord, thank you for making me a woman. Thank you for giving me life. Thank you for choosing me to be a helper, Lord. I pray and give thanks in Jesus' name. Amen.

About the 3rd Piece
From Black Son to Mother

A friend once told me he was taught that a foolish son comes from a foolish mother. It was a shocking revelation but it was true. At some point a mother has to let her son go and respect his manhood. She must also try not to turn her son into a man too soon when he is a child by loading him with awesome responsibilities. A son and daughter should be taught properly, in proper time. A son is meant to flourish into a man to take care of his family and be a provider. He can't blossom into his purpose if he is too attached to his mother.

From Black Son To Mother

Woman, do you see what stands before you?
Do you actually see?
Here before you stands a man; a real man, a Black Man!

Strong, confident, brave, intelligent, and beautiful
Because I like it that way
And because that is how I was taught to be

Do not be angry at my impatience, I am eager to learn
Don't rush my speech, I think before I speak

I am a magnificent being bore by you
I have reached boundaries others dare not soar
Climbed walls many tire of too soon
Pushed past barriers few came close to penetrating

I am the Black Son
Do you hear me? Are you here with me?

Yes, my opinions are strong, whether right or wrong
Don't stop me now; let me finish now. Hear me out
Scream, "Speak it, brother!" when I shout
Don't hush me

If I am lacking in my facts tell me later, don't hurt my pride
Give me time to accept true knowledge and take it in stride
No one is born ignorant
Through a failure to know or show, it is taught
Teach me differently
Allow my seeds to blossom and my fields to grow throughout

If you don't have the knowledge
Go and get the knowledge
For your sake and my sake

Like huge catfish in the sea

There should be no limits to my character
And no ceilings over me
For my mind is my key

I am the Black Son
By the mother, from whence I come
I stand proud under the father
And second to no one
I shall not be out done

My woman loves me; she says I have a wide mouth
She loves to hear me laugh and what comes out
She says I am beautiful
She steadily reminds me of what I already know
She loves me from my charcoaled fingertips
To my bronze covered toes

My features are distinct, very exaggerated, and extreme
To make even the dumbest understand who I am
And the purpose of what my position means

My brothers fall weak sometimes
But you taught me not to bash or smash
What appears to be trash
But pick it up and make treasure out of it and so I am
And those I cannot take with me
I leave the message of who I am
And what they should strive to be

I am the Black Son

You should never see me without a good book
Without a wide grin or without my good looks
I triumph over all, in whatever I do or whatever I speak
I am the mountain's peak

Don't hurt my pride and quiet me
Say preach brother, preach son, PREACH!

They've tried incarcerating my body
But still they could not hang or chain me
My body was numbed by the Father!
He has freed thee!
He knows what I am; marvelous, birthed by you
My impact may be vast but my kind is very few

I am from jungles of gold, soils of rich
Lands of plenty and colors of pitch
The Lord made me so dark, so from heaven he could see
The wonderful piece of perfection he created, easily

Though the battle is not over
From the beginning I've already won
Woman do you see this glorious man, child before you?
I am the Black Son!

Time to Cut the Apron Strings

This poem was written for my brothers, fathers, and sons. I had a friend who was going through some problems with his mother. While he was struggling to be independent, she was still trying to hold on to him. He couldn't get her to understand that he was trying to save his money so he could move out on his own. He found out that she was further behind on her bills than she mentioned and needed him to give her even more money. So, he was frustrated. He felt like she was not only in his pocket but in his business as well. His mom was depending on him too much. He needed to move out on his own in order for her to see him as the man he was. It was impossible for her to separate her son from the man he was becoming because he was still under her roof. So, all she saw was her child, a little boy.

Sometimes, mothers can be overbearing and not realize it. I think we often forget that our children are now adults, even under our roof. Sometimes mothers forget their sons are just sons and not their man. A mother's emotional attachment to her son may be seen as normal but at a certain point it has to be limited or cut. After a while, it can become bothersome for both parties, especially when communication is lacking. It can either make the son a burden in relationships with women because he feels the need to be babied or continuously puts his mother first. Or he can become very controlling because he feels like he is in a constant battle to prove his manhood.

This poem is also about the way some women view black men. It was written as an outcry for the unleashing of the black man. It's imperative that a woman learns to respect a man's views (not necessarily agree with them all but respect them) and how to love him correctly. This means listening to him, challenging him in a positive way, complimenting him, praising him, encouraging him, and learning to be honest with him in a very compassionate way. In other words, do not dog the man out or holler at him like he is a child. If he is immature and you are in a relationship with him, what does that really say about you? Either help him to get to the next level or leave him be but don't make him worse.

Any man who is silly enough not to love a sister that respects his manhood is definitely a fool. And, nobody likes or respects a fool.

Read this poem to your man and tell him how beautiful he is. Praise him for his goodness and thank God for bringing him to you. Make him feel like a man. This isn't kissing up. It is appreciating him and learning how to love him for who he is and what he stands for.

If you have a son, tell him this poem is about him.

If you are married, read, and discuss this poem with your husband. Afterwards, share which qualities listed within this poem that remind you of him. I can almost guarantee you the best sex you have had in a while. Then, in the morning, cook him some one-eyed jacks. Heck, he might want to cook some for you!

One-Eyed Jacks

2-4 slices of bread
2-4 eggs
1 tablespoon of butter/margarine/olive oil
Seasonings: salt and pepper

1. Melt butter in medium non-stick frying pan
2. Take a half-dollar size hole out of bread slice and place remaining slice in pan
3. Crack egg open into center of the bread.
4. Add seasonings
5. After egg white has cooked on the bottom or bread is golden, flip bread, and egg
6. Now cook for 30-45 seconds until new side is done

*Do not cook yoke completely
*Serve with rice or grits, bacon, turkey or sausage, and applesauce
*Don't forget a glass of orange juice or milk
*Men like this unique breakfast; it is healthy and fulfilling

Servings: 2
Prep & Cook time: 5 minutes

<u>Suggest Scriptures:</u>
Titus 2:2
1 Peter 5:5
1 Timothy 3:2-7
1 Corinthians 11:12, 13:11
Ephesians 5:31 and 33
Psalm 139, 14-16
Genesis 1:26-27
Acts 17: 26-28
Jeremiah 1:9-10
Proverbs 15:20, 17:25

Dear Lord,

Please bless the son in my life. Keep him covered and looking upwards to follow your lead. Lord, help him to make wise decisions and always choose you first. Bless him with the wisdom of you, his heavenly father. Bless his seeds so that his generations will grow to be strong, wise, God-fearing men and women. Lord, I also pray that you bless the husband and head of my household and that he always submits to your authority and seek you first in all that he does. Keep his intentions pure and good. I love you, Lord, the head of my life. Help me to build the man in my life up and encourage them to be the best. Thank you in Jesus' name. Amen.

About the 4th Piece
Strivers

We must instill confidence into our children while they are very young. They have to be taught to seek knowledge, learn respect, and give back to their community. The bible says that babies are selfish. They cry when they are hungry, want constant attention, and need your affection all the time. So, it is our responsibility to teach them how to be caring and share. Also, to show them right from wrong and introduce them to our creator, their true king!

Strivers

For me to make it is a must
And those who choose not to follow
I leave behind like dust in the wind
And blow them off like a gust
Because success is mine
And in time you will see
I was made to succeed
So strivers should heed
And store knowledge in the heads of the hollow
I was made not to follow but lead
And to my people add good deeds
I pick up heads of shame
And in their brains, engrave my name
I am headed for fame
Can't you see it?
You investing in me is like investing into your life
You get out of it
What you put into it
And I am money well spent
And life well lived
The recycler to many
Because back to my people I give—
Knowledge, experience, character, and growth overall
Not only do I strive to build me up
I strive to nurture us all
Strivers, strive…constantly.

Hold Your Head Up High and Keep Going!

Strivers is a poem that I believe every child needs to hear and live by. I wrote this poem and sent it to a Black Organization for a scholarship, I didn't get it. But, the poem has still inspired so many people despite that fact. I always wondered if I didn't get the scholarship because the poem appeared too cocky and confident but that's another story.

These words are meant to instill values of confidence and self-worth into the reader. The purpose is to open young minds to the realization that they can achieve anything they strive for. If they make a mistake, they can get up, dust off, and keep going. I also wanted parents to realize the importance of investing into their children's future.

Sometimes we don't know our self-worth. God has blessed each of us with a gift because we really are just that important to Him. It's painful to see young people go through life thinking they don't matter. That is a large reason why so many suffer abuse at the hands of others and themselves.

We all have a mission in life. We all have something inside of us that can affect humankind in a positive way. The objective is to figure out your mission and complete it. The good life is not just meant for some people and not others. Everyone has an opportunity to accomplish their dreams but it takes lots of courage, prayer, and faith. Most successful people had no clue they would end up that way or how. However, their courage, determination, and actions finally made it happen. God doesn't give anyone anything that will do harm. He blesses us with things to make us better. It doesn't always seem that way but it is true. How many times have you heard stories about someone born with a severe handicap using what may be considered a weakness to help others find strength and encouragement?

Again, it is up to us to make the choice of whether or not we want to use the tools we have to become the success we want to be. No matter what background or horrible circumstance we come from, there is always chance and forever hope. When neither of those seems to be enough, we can always rejoice at the fact that there most certainly is tomorrow. And although tomorrow isn't promised to us, we can still hope for it to be better for somebody else. Until God brings it all to an end, our duty is to keep striving.

This poem was the pledge of The Future Leader Reader Newspaper, a publication I started for children when I was only 22. But I began dreaming about it when I was just twelve. All of the paper's subscribers were encouraged to read it and live by it. I hope you are inspired to do the same.

No Wrong Way Spaghetti

1 can of mushrooms or 5 fresh mushrooms chopped
1 green pepper
1 onion
2 tablespoons of minced garlic
3 tablespoons of butter or margarine
1 pound of ground beef or turkey
1 pound of Italian sausage (optional)
1 16-ounce can of diced tomatoes
3 16-ounce cans of tomato sauce
1 can of water
1 6-ounce can of tomato paste
16 ounces of spaghetti
Seasonings: salt, pepper, red seasoning salt, rosemary, oregano

1. Place large pot of water with a teaspoon of salt on stove to boil
2. Chop green peppers and onions into small squares
3. Place green peppers, onions, garlic, and mushrooms in small saucepan, cover and simmer for 10 minutes
4. Lightly season meat, cook, and drain any fat
5. Place meat and vegetable mixture in medium pot and mix with tomatoes and seasonings. Simmer for 15 minutes
6. Pour sauce and drained spaghetti in the larger pot
7. Simmer all of the ingredients for 10 minutes and Whala!

*Serve with garlic bread and/or salad

Servings: 6-8
Prep & Cook time: 1:10 minutes

<u>Suggested Scriptures:</u>
Psalm 78:1-8
Proverbs 22:6, 23:24-25
Psalms 127:3-4
2 Timothy 1:5-7
Mark 10:13-15

Dear Lord,

Please help us to protect the children and keep them safe from harm. Help them to learn your ways, Lord. You said, "My sheep know my voice." Show them the correct way in this world of craziness and ungodliness. Help them to be givers and not takers, community builders, and not destroyers. Let us as parents, elders, and authority figures be good role models. Lord, keep our children focused on you. Please open their minds to the limitless possibilities of your love. Assure them that with you all things are possible because nothing is impossible for you, Lord. Fill them with your love so that they can exemplify a good life. I pray and ask all these things in the name of Jesus Christ. Amen.

About the 5th Piece
Families and Bonds

A family is a beautiful thing. Not only is it your bloodline; it is also your lifeline. Things like money, greed, jealousy, and envy can destroy a family. That is why it is important to learn how to forgive, look out for each other's best interests and take care of each other. So, if you have a dispute with someone you love, resolve it quickly and peacefully. The bible warns us not to sleep on our wrath. We aren't promised tomorrow. So, have faith and don't put off anything that you can do today. If the other person doesn't want to let go, you can rest easy knowing you sought to resolve the issue. Hopefully, they will eventually come around, too.

Families & Bonds

What keeps us strong going, on and on
Focused and moving and bonding bonds
Tightening, heightening, lighting the way
For days of praise and life's twisting maze
That glues tight glorious fights til' doom for family looms
And hearts that bloom
To bring forth seeds of laughter
Before and after
And tightens grips on finger tips and moistens hardened lips
To speak and say, "I'm sorry," before it's too late
And hate disrupts fate to turn into a disaster
Of stubborn pride's evil rapture?
What rips apart a family's heart and leaves stones
Cold to touch and numb to feel, easy to die and hard to kill?
What element could be so clever and quick
To pick apart at the very heart and soul of the essence
Of families and bonds causing more harm than help
Emptying promises for none to be kept?
Should the good just walk away or sway into the wind
Never to touch face again?
When the answer is quite simple...
Blood cannot be erased but traced by each who has its trait
Therefore it is and shall always be the matter
You cannot change the past nor predict the future
But prepare for what comes next
And respect how it is to be...
You see? No battle fought and none won
When it comes to the breaking of Families and Bonds.

Blood Can Never Be Erased

This is the most controversial piece I've ever written. It was created two weeks before my Grandfather's death. I watched my family fall apart right in front of my face. I wanted to get the message across that no matter what happened we were blood and would always be family.

It seemed like as soon as the doctor stated that my grandfather might have cancer, the horror began. The first thing I remember someone saying was, "We need to create a living will." It seemed like everyone turned against my mother at once. Like they forgot that for three years after my grandmother's death who took care of him. She opened her home to him, while everyone else had their own reasons as to why they could not. They didn't even consider the fact that she never had any breaks or privacy. She saw him everyday, not just when it was convenient. She cooked for my grandfather, bathed him and she didn't make him feel helpless because she allowed him to be independent. He cooked when he wanted to, went for walks and did whatever else he desired because she respected him as a father and his manhood. Instead of being a lifesaver, however, she was soon portrayed as a deceitful daughter out for his money. My mother took care of my Grandfather because she loved him and nothing more. My stepfather wouldn't even accept any money from Mudaddy, my grandfather, because he said it was our responsibility to take care of him now.

The family decided to move Mudaddy into his own apartment even though the doctor only gave him a few months to live. They thought they were giving him what he always wanted. I could not figure out how they came to that conclusion considering his 48 years of marriage to my grandmother. They were together since she was sixteen. I figured if he wanted to live on his own, he would have left years ago. I really think some of my family members were in denial and didn't want to accept what was really happening. He could hardly walk because of his hospital operation; he barely could lift his left arm, which was a drawback from the stroke. So, I'm pretty sure he didn't want to be alone.

This moment in my family's life was so heartbreaking. It was the first time I ever saw Mudaddy cry. After he came home from the hospital, they brought him to my mom's to collect the rest of his belongings. When they pulled up to the house, he kept trying to get out of the car but they wouldn't let him. They told him it wasn't his home anymore. My grandfather just broke down crying. I believe his hurt was ignored because no one really wanted to accept that we were going to lose him, the matriarch of our family. Denial can cause so much pain.

Before moving my grandfather out, they had my mom put his bank account in some of their names. At this point, it was decided that it would be necessary so everyone could get a fair share of any money he might have. My grandfather was very disappointed and they knew it. I remember him sitting down and pointing forcefully at my mother, shaking his head, and telling her no. He did not want her to do it. She couldn't handle the pressure so she did what her siblings asked. His decisions were dismissed as him not thinking clearly. My mother was so hurt. She couldn't believe how the family she loved so much seemed to turn on her.

Suddenly, everyone had time to be around Mudaddy at his new place. It was sad because when he was well, no one seemed to have this much time. It seemed like everyone felt guilty and tried to soothe their conscious by doing something at the last minute. It's funny what death can really do to a family and it is not always the right thing.

Eventually, things really began to fall apart. They took Mudaddy's golden retriever, Goldie, away because it couldn't stay in the apartment with him. He really loved that dog. For as long as I can remember, my grandfather always kept a dog. It got so bad that my grandfather refused to eat unless my mother cooked his food. He was really upset with his children.

Some of my family members were upset with me for protecting my mother. But they were saying so many bogus things about her, even to me. I don't even think they realized the negative impact their allegations had on my siblings and I. We were hurt. They felt I should stay out of it because it wasn't my concern. Like it was just between them and not their children. I felt like I had a right to speak up, as long as I wasn't disrespectful. I was 25 years old and completely independent. Oh, I was entitled to my opinion because this issue concerning my mother was most certainly my business.

In large families, especially, it can be hard for elders to accept the fact that the younger generations are getting older and have a voice.

Well, my response to everyone's accusations was, "If you thought she was doing all of these things, why didn't you speak up sooner?"

No one had an answer, of course. If it's two things I despise, it's liars and thieves. In this case, however, it was dishonesty and separation; especially, when it was coming from within my own family. This was a time in my life when my entire family needed a bunch of prayer.

At one point, my mom was so disturbed with everything going on that she got very drunk and put a 9mm gun into her mouth. Thank God she didn't pull the trigger! That really showed me how much people can destroy your spirit. I just looked at this woman, whom I considered so strong, differently. I saw her in a whole new light. It was like she finally became human to me; instead of this immortal superwoman I had always thought her to be. I discovered that she was very fragile especially when it came to the people she really loved. She was only strong because she had to be. Without her family, it seemed like my mom was nothing.

The truth is not the prettiest thing sometimes. My mother was very hurt but I believe this experience opened her eyes to so much. Some things that she didn't see and some things that she just chose to ignore. At points, I honestly felt like she loved her siblings more than us. She would go out on a limb for them and leave us to be "strong". I guess it was good that she raised us to be survivors. Most kids grow up weak and resentful because of that. But we didn't; we grew up to be fighters and independent, no matter our circumstances.

I reminded her of what she taught me which was once I had a family, they became my number one priority and everyone else was secondary.

"You seem to have forgotten that. Maybe, God wanted you to see who had your back. You have to let them go. I know you love them but let them go and give it to God," I urged her.

Eventually, she did. She dusted herself off, recognized that she did all that she could do, and moved on. And, shortly after everything was over, everyone began coming back around. It started with phone calls here and a visit there until it was all brushed under the rug and back to normal, again.

It was interesting how different folks reacted when I read this poem at the funeral. First, I said a poem called "Grandfather's Hands", which was printed in the obituary. But, I also had the funeral home place an insert with both, My Word, My Words and Families and Bonds, in it. It was a shocker! Those who didn't understand the drama loved this poem. Those who knew what it meant were a little angry because they felt it was telling too much of our business. At that point, I realized I wrote the poem just right because my words struck a cord in some of them. I felt like God was moving my pen when I wrote it. Like God was allowing my grandfather to whisper his feelings into my mind and ears before he died. It needed to be said and heard.

Fortunately, no love was lost after the incident but trust was definitely shaken. Some of my family asked my mom why I said that poem at the funeral. My mom told me she just smiled and said, "Well, you know Meochia, she speaks her mind, just ask her." No one ever did.

My family finally reconciled; it didn't take too long. Everyone went back to normal, loving each other and visiting each other's homes for the holidays. My mom's house is still the one everyone likes to visit when they are in town. I guess we just had a bump in the road. The important thing is that we made it through. We still love each other although we did get a big dose of reality; we are not the perfect family. Oh my, really?!

Money can make you forget who you are, as well as, who your real friends and family are. Money brings things out and opens things up. Our hope is that good intentions don't turn into negative ones when it comes to it. In the bible it is considered the root of evil. That's why our families need to be rooted in God because He plants the good seeds. He designed the family tree and its structure in the beginning when he created the heavens and the earth. In the grander scheme of things, we are all one big family and each member is just a small stitch in God's great fabric of life, and nothing should separate us.

Black Folks Lasagna

½ pound of Italian sausage
1 pound of ground beef/turkey
16 ounces of sliced American cheese
16 ounces of sliced Swiss cheese
16 ounces of shredded mozzarella cheese
16 ounces of shredded sharp cheddar
2 cups of Parmesan cheese
24 ounces of tomato sauce
1 can of diced tomatoes
½ cup of mushrooms, green peppers, onions,
(spinach, optional)
1 tablespoon of fresh garlic
1 teaspoon of oregano
2 tablespoons of margarine
1 package of lasagna shells

1. Preheat oven to 350°
2. Mix, season and cook Italian sausage and ground beef
3. Melt margarine in a saucepan and add oregano, minced green peppers, mushrooms, sliced garlic, and onions. Let simmer for 10 minutes
4. Add tomato sauce, diced tomatoes, and vegetables to the meat mixture
5. In a large pot boil lasagna shells until done, place in cold water to cool
6. Be careful when lifting shells because they tear easily
7. First, place layer of shells into a baking pan
8. Next add meat sauce and spinach
9. Then, layer shredded cheeses and Parmesan, American, Swiss cheese, and Cottage cheese
10. Repeat process again starting with lasagna shells; this should make two or three layers
11. Top with shredded cheese and meat sauce
12. Place lasagna in the oven for 30 minutes (If you leave in too long it may become soupy or hard on top)

*Serve with broccoli, salad or asparagus, and garlic bread

Servings: 6+
Prep & Cook time: 1½ hours

<u>Suggested Scriptures</u>
Romans 8:37-39
1 Timothy 5:7-8
Colossians 3:12-15
Hebrews 2:14
Proverbs 1:19, 15:27

Dear Lord,

Please bring peace upon my family and I. Let us be friends, as well, family; and family, as well as, friends. Give us harmony and resolution, Lord. Please allow nothing to come in and separate us from the love of each other, just as nothing or no one can separate us from your love. Keep our hearts filled with forgiveness, our mouths overflowing with praise, and our eyes fixed on you, Lord. I pray and ask all these things in Jesus' name. Amen.

About the 6th Piece
Black Woman with a Grudge

Both parents share the responsibilities of raising a child. Children don't ask for perfect parents; they just require love and plenty of it. God loves and protects children. His warnings are clear about anyone who dares to harm them. As mothers, we should not hate our children's father. Instead we should focus on helping them to become better people, if they are open to receive it. We should be confident in the Lord. We worship a Great God who is the definition of Agape Love. He is the Almighty God and with Him all things are possible. When we turn our focus toward Him, nothing or no one can get in our way of success and greatness. So, sisters lets be slow to anger and quick to forgive like the bible instructs us. We have to show our daughters how to be compassionate nurturers and our sons how to be leaders and protectors.

Black Woman With A Grudge

And you all ask me why, when you squawk, I sigh?
Because on all those opinions I do not rely
Ask myself, "Is it truth or a lie?"
Yeah, I am fine but any sister will do
Sure, he's different but I saw him look, too!
Hats off to the married man but isn't that a big lie
Sure, those are the ones to get but they've aced being sly

If you don't speak, you're stuck up
If you do, you're a bore
If you happen to care for one
They don't love you no more...
It could be your first time; it could be your last
But get it girl to the sister who gave it all a pass!
You brothers trippin' like we aren't good enough for you
Pretty, ugly, educated, dumb, rich or poor
You're gonna do what you are going to do

It isn't her who makes you; it's you who makes yourself
Go on out there and act a fool
You are just another trophy on my shelf
For the "Broke Down Brotha" Award
Get mad or upset, I'm a black woman with a grudge
Attack me with your brutal strength
And I bet you I won't budge
I have had enough and my sisters have, too
We are going to have to struggle together
And learn to just step around you

We're tired of begging for help
Asking Uncle Sam to support your kids
You're walking around in Nikes
While we're still wearing skids
Keep your girlfriends carrying Visa
The closes your kids see is Link
Before she lay down with you, the sister better think!

Having a fit because we want a single brother with money No
more than a child or two
Who's about getting his education and not acting a fool
You all trapped most of us with that young love
You men can start again
When we want to go for better
You would think we committed a sin

My child isn't going to want for anything
What Daddy won't do I will
I won't disrespect you but I tell you time kills
You can do your thing now
But I'm getting it together and pulling things apart
I am starting over fresh by first emptying my heart
I'm placing new cards on the table
Doing what I have to do
My children are crying now
But when they're older, you're going to be through
I'll leave that part up to you, them, and God
You see, I'm headed for blessed days
I am opening myself up for true love to pass my way
Skip them other flavors, I'm still hoping for some fudge
Excuse me, brothers, for venting
I'm just a black woman with a grudge!

It Takes Two To Make Them and Raise Them

Baby Daddy drama is an understatement! I was tired of men, altogether. I wrote this as an outcry for mothers, girlfriends, single, and married women. There is no one right way to satisfy a man. A man could have a beautiful woman and cheat on her with an ugly one. He could have a slim woman, talk negatively about a fat one, and end up with a huge one. Some will speak disapprovingly about strippers and prostitutes and be the first one in the club paying one. Or be caught on television with one in their car.

This piece was like a personal vendetta against my own child's father at the time. I believe we both have matured a lot since then. I can't understand why some men seem satisfied when a woman is struggling, single, and taking care of their children. However, when she is doing great, involved, and asking for support; they think she has lost her mind. It makes you beg to ask the questions:

"Now, why would I let you get away with not supporting your child just because I have my own money?"

"We both lied down and had this child together. Why would I or any other mother let you off without an ounce of responsibility or liability?"

Both parents should be involved and/or paying to support their children.

Some women get so wrapped up in that independent stuff and they forget that the extra cash helps. Plus, the children deserve it. If a woman doesn't need the money, she can put it into a savings account for the child's future. Not accepting his money is not hurting him. It is helping him become more irresponsible by spending it on someone else, possibly, to make another baby. So take what is yours. When he screams that he is having money problems, tell him his child is, too.

Now listen, there is a flip side to this. I don't want it to be misunderstood or for anyone to think that I am male bashing or telling sisters to hurt a brother. Totally, not! There are some really good men out there who cannot afford to take care of their children the way they desire. Just like there are some sisters out there who have fallen on hard times. Men don't have it as easy as women because the majority of us have residential custody and the government has more programs that can assist women. But even the amount of help from the government is not enough all the time.

So, if your child's father is truly struggling and he's a good guy, you should cut him a break. But he should still be spending time with his child and helping out as much as he can.

I actually went a complete year without receiving benefits from my child's father so that he could get back on his feet. When he did get himself together, he paid arrears. My job wasn't to kill my daughter's father or make him feel worse. So, I tried to be as patient and understanding as I could be at the time.

Filing for support is simple. It doesn't cost if you file pro bono or get assistance through your state. Also, you can do it your self. When you go through the courts, independently, your chances of getting more financial help increases versus going through the government. Plus, it keeps the both of you out of the system. But when you go through the government, there is a state record of every financial transaction, you get free representation and mediation, and it protects both of your records and payments.

Most men hate being in the system. And I can't say I blame them too much. But, if he is not handling your situation right, file! Forget that stuff about keeping the government out of your business. It will benefit both of you in the future. You do not need his social security number. Go to the child support centers in your city and get the paperwork to file. Get three copies of your court papers and send a certified copy to him with return receipt. Make sure you have payments sent through the city, first; this is for both his and your protection. Just tell your child's father that you are looking out for your child's best interest. If he needs a blood test give him one, it will be billed to him, anyway (depending upon your state). And I hope you know it is his for sure. "You are not the father" seems to be the phrase of the century. This whole process may take about two months. Make sure you keep all your court records in order within some type of binder (judges like it when you are well organized). If you misplace any records the child support agency should have a copy that you can use and make copies from whenever necessary. Mothers, please get educated!

After writing this piece, I realized how frustrated I was and how much I needed to let go of my own anger. I felt betrayed. I also noticed how many women feel hopeless and helpless living the single life. It sets up a state of confusion. You don't know whether to be caring or daring. You are faced with a broken family and home. This is a consequence of our own sin but God is good and he provides redemption!

Now, what I have also discovered through my own faults is that men put women on a certain pedestal. And, the only person that can take her off of it is herself. That means you must stick to your guns, your values, and your morals. You cannot let go of who you are to please a man. Once you do, he starts seeing you differently. Now, you may lose a lot of guys this way but the right guy will stay and respect you for being a woman of virtuous character. You also have to learn to "take the garbage out". That means you must let go of past drama and give each new person a chance. Also, you must give yourself a chance to try again. Your child deserves the best and so do you.

And remember, being single is just as cool as being in a relationship. So don't rush it, enjoy some time with yourself and with your children if you have any.

Low-Budget String Beans

5 slices of bacon or smoked turkey parts
2 potatoes
1 medium onion
3 cans of string beans or 1½ pounds of fresh string beans chopped
Seasonings: salt, pepper

1. Fry bacon and slice into one inch squares or boil turkey for 30-45 minutes
2. Square-cut potatoes
3. Square cut onion
4. Drain, rinse, and place beans in medium pot with 3 cans or cups of water
5. Add all of the ingredients to the pot and seasonings
6. Cover and place on low-medium heat for 1½ hours
7. Stir every 20 minutes

Servings: 4-6
Prep & Cook time: 2 hours

<u>Suggested Scriptures</u>
Psalms 10:1-18
Colossians 3:12-14
Matthew 6:12
Proverbs 26:4-5
1 Corinthians 13:4-7; 7:32-35
1 John 4:7-18
1 Timothy 5:8

Dear Lord,

Please open up my heart to forgiveness and passion. Lord, bless me with your sight to see beyond what is in front of me now so that I may look to the bigger picture in the future. Lord, bless my child with a strong mind, a heart of love, and eyes that are wise. Let my child(ren) know that no matter what they are going through, you love them, Lord. Help them to see that no matter where they are or what they have done, you are there, Lord. For every disappointment they may face, you will provide light, love, and a way. Lord, bless my child's father. Keep him safe Lord. Help him to recognize and follow you, Lord. Lord, there is nothing like a man who submits to You. If he seeks you first, Lord, he will walk in righteousness thereby leading his children to a good and healthy future. Lord, bless us as parents so that our little ones will suffer no harm. Help us to appreciate and honor your gifts. Lord, you have given these children to us as little gifts to be treasured and to worship you. Thank you, Lord in Jesus' name. Amen.

About the 7th Piece
Settling For It

Each of us has a gift and purpose for being on this earth. Regardless of how many you have or what your gift is, it is your duty to bless the world with it. You must live your life to the fullest and not let anyone steal your shine. It is not wise to allow anyone to take away your dreams. But the great thing about our precious God is that whatever he has for you is for you only and no one can take it away. However, you can forfeit your promise by not living out your purpose. So drop the drama and get on with your life. You have an appointment with God!

Settling For It

Craving that success light, waiting for the time that's right
Thinking in the middle of the night
How you should just take flight
Air is lost if you leave but if you stay you still can't breathe
Step on faith and take heed
PRAY for the strength that you need

Settle to dismiss that change of heart
While your life just falls apart
Want to make a brand new start
But you're as good at guessing as you are at art
Following second when first mind is telling you to go
Listening to others tell you answers you already know
If truth flows through the knows and nostrils of the old
Let it unfold but the only one you know never told
Because he can't talk
So you walk and you walk, falling down, asking, praying, saying:
HELP ME TO HOLD ON
While your life is laying-- on the edge of a split decision
Waiting for that vision
Craving to break free of this mental prison
Keeping your lips sealed while you listen
For that special phrase; that special sentence
That is going to pep you up to start again
To say you are not alone, you have friends
And ask you, "Why are you settling?"

Destiny only has one choice FULFILLMENT
And you or I can't STOP IT
So that baggage DROP IT
That next train HOP IT
This mountain TOP IT
When you have it and God gave it
It never dies but lies within you
Waiting for your next move
So stop settling when more is available

Engulf it; the world is yours
Not just one piece, swallow it whole!

Only Dust Is Allowed to Settle

Settling For It is about getting your life back on track. I've heard so many people talk about how smart, beautiful, rare, and good they are. But, on the inside, if you look deep enough, you can tell they are crying for help. It takes an experienced woman to recognize that facade. Otherwise, you'll be fooled like the rest. I had other people convinced that I had it together, too. However, I was still putting up with things that I should not have. It was like I was scared to let go and start over. I couldn't blame anyone because I chose each of my paths. So one night I made up my mind that I should just pack up and leave my current life, not town. And I did.

I had finally reached a point in my life where I felt like I did not have to answer to anyone except God. I must admit this attitude was not easy to come by. It is hard trying to convince yourself to put your foot down when you are the one who chose to have it up in the first place. But you have to have a breaking point when you say enough is enough and I will not take it anymore. Just write a list of things you need versus things you want and have. When you are finished, review your list, and then ask yourself, "Why am I settling?"

You need to have a plan in life, a vision, and some goals set. You need a roadmap that you can always refer back to and make sure you are staying on track. Don't allow yourself to get sidetracked and don't ever backtrack. We get caught up in blaming others for our own misfortune when it really boils down to ourselves. If you don't like the current state your life is in, change it! Of course, you cannot do it all in one day but with God all things are possible. Everything takes time. So stop beating yourself up and take your time. Everything has a process. Remember that a baby drinks liquids first, then baby food, and finally, solid foods. Learning to do one thing at a time is much easier than doing nothing at all. So, get moving!!!

Shut Yo' Mouth Cube Steak

3 pounds of cubed steak
1 large red and green pepper (cut in large squares)
1 large onion (cut in large square chunks)
Seasonings: salt, pepper, seasoning salt, onion powder
1/3 cup of olive oil
1 cup of flour
Frying pan

1. Warm oil in large frying pan on medium heat
2. Clean steak and season both sides lightly
3. Coat each steak with flour to avoid sticking
4. Place patties in frying pan and cook for 4 minutes on each side or until both have a thin crust
5. Remove from pan and place on paper towel to drain
6. Pour most of the grease out of the pan
7. Add tablespoon of flour to prepare a gravy
8. Add a cup of water and more seasoning
9. As gravy thickens add vegetables and cook for 5 minutes.
10. Add more flour for thicker gravy or more water to thin the gravy
11. Add all the patties to the gravy, turn heat to low, and cover
12. Cook for 12 minutes on each side. Occasionally stir to mix gravy and ensure even coverage of patties

*Serve over rice with favorite vegetable and biscuits

Servings: 4-6 patties
Prep & Cook time: 1 hour

<u>Scriptures</u>
Philippians 4:13
Proverbs 20:5 and 13
Romans 8:31-32
Jeremiah 1:5, 29:11

Dear Lord,

Help me discover my purpose in life so that I may walk in it. Help me to get out of my own way so that I can walk into the destiny you have planned for my life. Lord, give me vision, give me knowledge, and give me wisdom and stamina. I need staying power, Lord. Lord, shake off the chains of procrastination, contentment, and fear because these are not of you. Put wise people in my life who can help me reach my goals. Let your will be done in my life and allow me to stay focused on your light and deeply rooted in your word. Do not let me forfeit my blessings. Lord, invest in me, plant your seeds of righteousness in my heart so that I can be a shining example of what being steadfast in the Lord is all about. Oh thank you for all of my talents and gifts. I do not want to be like the man in the bible who buried his. I want to be like the man who multiplied all his talents by two and prospered. I want to multiply your gifts onto others so that they may seek your glory and know that you are God the Almighty. Oh, thank you for everything righteous father and thank you for making me a vessel. You are glorious, you are great, you are perfect, you are the great giver, and the great multiplier. You are all I ever need and more. I just thank you Father in Jesus' name. Amen.

About the 8th Piece
Wake My People

Just as God took the children of Israel out of bondage, he can rescue you from any form of slavery. No matter what has a grip on your life: drugs, sex, spousal abuse, molestation, negativity, drama, or depression, God can take you out of it. You just have to follow and trust in Him. If you have faith in Him and stay the course, you will be delivered! Sometimes it may seem slow to you but God will always come through. It's all a part of the process of making you better. You are not a product of your environment; you are a rare treasure within it!

Wake My People

Hey my people don't you have anything else to
Write about, Talk about, Speak about, Walk about?

The are still calling you "niggas"
Spreading your streets with triggers
Dominating you in figures

Some things haven't changed like some of them
Stealing from him
From white sheets to brims

College statistics show change
From monkeys to brains
But from slave chains to gangs

Hey my people don't you have something to
March about, Dream about, Shout about?

We choose to snooze but those who sleep lose
We still living in the 60's
Sisters getting abused
Brothers being used to inflict her bruises

We hide under our beds like a leech
Being blinded by what they teach
Instead of exercising our right to free speech
Still, scared say, "Don't talk...
If there's a march, I won't walk!"
Well the bible says if that eye is causing you to sin
Then cut it out
So take out that mouth if you are not going to shout
Because a whisper cannot be heard

"Nothing's changing," you say but you won't vote
While your children are filled with marijuana and dope
Scared to take a stance for justice

Won't even lick and mail an envelope

Bringing drugs and guns into our communities
Filling our brothers with bullets and our sisters with disease
Swarming around us like bees with monies
Come time to pay the bills, run like a dog with fleas

Years ago we were killed for knowing words
Ink was our death now lead has us dead

But to speak is my freedom and with it I will kill
My God is my strength, my heart is my will

My people don't you have someone to
Boost about, to Stand about, to Vote about?

Hey my people you have rights to
Speak about, to Walk about, to March about!

Hey my people when are you going to Stand up
Put you Hand up
Put your foot down
Bring those clowns down
Take back your town?

Hey my people stand up before it's too late
Change can't wait
King died because of hate

This our month, this is our year, these are our days
No one has to stand for a man's evil ways

What won't kill you will only make you stronger
Vote, vote, vote…if you won't take this any longer!

It's Time To Remove the Veil

I absolutely love the story behind this poem. I can honestly say that my mouth finally got me into trouble. During the 1999 mayoral election in my old town, I was arrested. It was in February during Black History Month. The mayor, who was white, said one of the representatives looked like a big, black monkey during a town hall meeting. That racist comment caused a lot of people to get upset and walk out.

One older lady stood up out of her chair and asked the mayor to apologize and of course he ignored her. But, she wouldn't sit down. Next thing you know, a young, black police officer, who had to be about 6'6, began shouting at her, telling her to shut-up and get out. In my opinion, he was just rude. I can understand a brother doing his job but I couldn't understand the disrespect of an elder. So, I stood up and told him that this was a public meeting and she had a right to speak. Of course, he began telling me to just shut up and get out, too.

Well, I did not even get a chance to shut up! Before I knew it, he was putting me under arrest. I wanted to know why I was being arrested. It was a public meeting and in public meetings the public has a right to voice their opinions. He came over and pushed me. I explained to him that I could walk perfectly fine and he didn't need to touch me because a female officer was present. He just ignored me and pushed me three more times. He pushed me so hard the last time that I fell on the floor and hit my face. He picked me up by my arm and escorted me out of the door. Then, two more police assisted him in cuffing me. Now, I am not really sure why it took two additional officers to help him with a woman. But, it could have been my grandfather's famous "Indian Bow Stance" that I tried to imitate.

Now, here's the story behind the "Indian Bow Stance":

My mom said my grandfather got arrested one time but the cops couldn't get him to sit up in the car. It all started when one of my uncles hit the neighbor in the head with a rock. When my grandmother took him to apologize for what he did, the man cursed her out and pushed her. When my grandfather found out what happened, he went across the alley and punched the man in the face.

So, the man yelled, "I'll just turn the other cheek!" So, my grandfather punched him in that one, too. Then, he beat the poor guy up. My mom said everyone ended up fighting in the alley that day.

Eventually, someone called the cops and my grandmother went to grab their shotgun. My grandparents may have had their differences but they sure did protect each other. Well, my auntie took the gun away from Mumomma so she wouldn't go to jail or shoot anybody and in turn, the police tried to arrest her. Now, Mudaddy wasn't about to let anyone in his family go to jail. So, he began tussling with the cops and they decided to arrest him, instead.

Momma said Mudaddy stood up straight with his legs slightly parted and his feet planted firmly; his upper body was bearing down on all of his weight. He stood in that stance and would not budge and nobody could move him. I can just imagine him standing there looking like a big Indian Chief statue. Four officers had to pick him up and put him in the car sideways. They had to ride with the windows open because they couldn't bend his legs, either. How funny! We don't seem to experience those types of stories, anymore.

Actually, Mumomma and Mudaddy's alley was the scene of a lot of family fights. They were exciting but in looking back, it's a good thing no one ever got killed. But I did get hit in the mouth with a two-by-four during one of those alley squabbles when I was little. I ended up with 15 stitches in my top lip and crooked teeth.

See, the younger children were always told to go in the house when a fight would start brewing. But, being the mischievous kids we were, we'd either peek out the windows of the attic and utility room; or, we'd sneak around to the front door and run back outside. We didn't want to miss any of the action. Well, that disobedience got me popped right in the mouth. What can I tell you?

But it was funny seeing countless men and women being passed from sibling to sibling in brawls that seemed to last all day. Back in those days, people mostly fought with their hands.

Anyway, back to the story about my arrest. After their sad attempt at cuffing me, they put me a patty wagon and drove me to the police station. They never discovered that only one of my hands was actually cuffed. I had to take a mug shot and get fingerprinted. I noticed that a different police officer came in and handled the report. He signed it as if he was making a complaint against me. I asked him where he came from because he wasn't even there. And he said he was just doing his job.

"It's a good thing they didn't tell you to shoot me," I said.

He explained that he was not like the other officers and that he didn't agree with what happened. I guess if you can't beat it, you might as well join it, huh?

Well, they charged me with trying to stir up a riot and disorderly conduct. The report said that I was cursing and screaming; these are things that would be considered loitering. Now, I did get a chance to study media law at Columbia College in Chicago and general law during a summer pre-law session at John Marshall Law School, as well. So, I knew they were trying to disguise the truth by exaggerating and lying. I did not deserve to get arrested but I think they needed to cover their butts for pushing me on the floor. It also explained why the mayor signaled for the media crew to turn off the cameras during the incident.

They finally released me after somebody posted my bond. When I came out into the station's lobby I saw almost 200 people flooding their waiting room demanding for me to be released. It was wonderful. And, I was commended for being brave and speaking out.

However, after the people marched one time, the crowd and the motivation all seemed to die out very quickly. The politicians concentrated on the racial slur that the mayor denied and glossed over the issue of police brutality.

I was harassed for months by someone calling my house and hanging up. So, I confronted the mayor in front of his house one day while he was out jogging. He was shocked when he found out I was the lady in the hat who was arrested that day. After all, he had just given me a small stipend to support my newspaper a month earlier. Nevertheless, he nonchalantly told me to just plead guilty. I said I don't think so. Instead, I summoned every alderman, who was present the day of the incident and the mayor's opponent, to court. I also wrote an article in a local newspaper describing the details of what happened. My cousin Bonnie always said, "There's your story and his story!"

Well, none of the officers ever appeared for trial and all the charges were dropped. People began warning me to be careful. But, I felt I had to stand up to the city and behind the Lord. I felt untouchable for a moment but soon reality hit. That same mayor won the election in a 91% black town, again. Some say he cheated but I don't think so. He would've had to cheat a whole lot.

I can remember saying this poem right before the voting date. People screamed, shouted, and even cried at such a strong poem. I just wished it could have reached more ears.

The mayor lost the following election. Sadly, he was diagnosed with cancer several years later and died. God bless his soul.

My story happens all over the world, everyday. More people need to read, write, speak to the right people (local politicians and state representatives), voice their opinions, and educate children about what is right and just. We sit down too much, talk on the phone too much, watch TV too much, complain too much, hate too much, and talk amongst ourselves too much. We stand together, too little. Laugh together too little, respect each other too little, compliment each other too little, put out surveys too little, start block clubs too little, go too church too little, and take church home too little. Pray too little and live by faith too little.

I am a true witness and believer of faith. I know God will not let anything happen to his people because he is an invisible shield of protection. That little piece of hang-on strength is all you need for him to pull you through. If you ever want to know if someone trusts you, you have to be willing to trust. If they give up on you, try your best not to give up on them. If you have been let down a lot trust can be very hard but practice it, anyway. That is how faith is. Sometimes waiting on God can be scary. But it is all about the process. You have to hold on, stand strong, and keep the faith. So wake up my people the morning has come!

Three Flavored Greens

2 stalks of greens: collard, mustard, turnip, and kale (optional)
2 big yellow onion
2 turnips, thinly sliced
4 smoked turkey parts
1 stick of butter
1 jalapeño pepper minced (optional)
3 boxes of baking soda to clean greens
Seasonings: salt, pepper, seasoning salt

1. Boil turkey parts and seasoning in a huge, deep pot of water for about an hour
2. Cut Collard greens across about 1 inch apart
3. Peel mustard and turnip greens off their stems
4. (Do not chop greens up unless you just like them that way)
5. Place the greens in warm water
6. Clean and rinse them three times with baking soda (Greens are clean when the dirt and water is clear)
7. Next add the greens to the seasoned boiling water
8. If the water is too high, empty some into a bowl for later (Some water may evaporate. If too low, add more)
9. Place all the greens in the pot and add onions, pepper, butter, and turnips
10. Cover and cook, stirring occasionally for 3 hours
11. Always check water level, not too high or too low
12. Cook for 3 hours

*If you like semi-rough textured greens do not cook over 3 hours
*If you would like mouth-watering greens and soft collards, cook for 4-5 hours.

Servings: 8+
Prep & Cook time: 4-5 hours

Suggested Scriptures
Leviticus 5:1
Matthew 5:29, 18:9
2 Chronicles 32:7-8, 21-22
Genesis 18:16-33

Dear Lord,

Please deliver my brothers and sisters from the many strongholds they may be struggling with. Lord, extend to them an open invitation to your loving grace. Help them with the chains that keep them enslaved and unable to truly experience what it is like to be born again. Let them experience true love, trust, honesty, and a help that asks for nothing but goodness and love in return. Lord, release my people from the bondage of discrimination, hate crimes, drugs, fornication, adultery, idolatry, self-hate, perversion, depression, and anything else that keeps them distracted and bound. Lord, draw them closer to you. Give them strength and courage to speak out against lawlessness. Bless them with a heart to listen, ears to hear, and eyes to see that you are the key to unlocking their misery. Keep their weary eyes focused on you, Lord, the Mighty Deliverer. I ask these things in Jesus' name. Amen.

Meochia Nochi Thompson

About the 9th Piece
To Our Mothers and Fathers

Parents have the great responsibility of setting a roadmap for their children. Which means that we are to lead by example. You cannot be an alcoholic and expect your child not to be tempted to drink or develop any addictions. So you must be careful of what you pour into them because you risk the possibility of them following in your footsteps. Be wise and show them the right way. Explain your decisions to them and allow them to express their concerns, as well. Remember, communication works two ways; each person must listen in order to receive. Support their ideas, encourage them to stand up for what is right and teach them how to fight with knowledge, maintain peace, and gain wisdom.

To Our Mothers and Fathers

To those people who encouraged me to be strong
And not succumb to wrong
To hold on when they let go
Said research, read, write, and listen to
What they don't even care to or are scared to know!
To those who let my generation down
Who lost us in the masses of a path they found
Who chose to snooze at a time that sleepers walk
And shined their lights for us to be caught
To our Mothers and Fathers who broke chains
Yet handed others reigns
Then instilled shackles upon our brains!
Those who covered their eyes refusing to look
While our powers were stolen by crooks
To those who mothered us and then smothered us
With visions they instilled
But couldn't fulfill because of their own jealousies
Pretending to care, falling to their knees
And hushing us when we stood to speak out
"Take out that mouth if you're not going to shout!"
We have visions and voices not illusions and noises
That are meant to be heard over shouts
If I stand you stand, don't fill me with doubts
It's not getting better mother
We aren't going further father
We're starving…
Malnourished thoughts our ancestors fed on and died of
Don't hush me to keep me alive just to die
Let me go to show love!

What Mama and Daddy Don't Know Could Hurt

I wrote this shortly after Wake My People. I noticed that some of the people in my family and neighborhood were scared of what might happen because I spoke out about the arrest. I couldn't believe it. I felt like I was in the 1960's ready to fight for freedom. What was everyone so afraid of? The bible says to fear God. It tells us not to fear death. I would rather die for change than live in shame. I wanted our parents to practice what our ancestors died for…freedom. I wanted our parents to see how hard we work to be brave for them, get educated for them, and speak out against wrong for them because there was a time when they couldn't.

Nowadays people want to hide behind the truth. Nobody wants to see the movies that portray slavery or racism. Or anything that speaks out against immoral behavior. We profess to be a contrite society but our actions show different. We don't want to offend anyone so we quietly sweep our views under a rug hoping no one will bring them up. Then, when someone does complain, we just say get over it or that's the past. I cannot pretend that discrimination didn't happen or doesn't exist because it happens everyday.

Now, are things getting better? Of course they are. America just voted in the first African-American President in 2008, Barack Obama. Was that a struggle? Of course it was. It was a hard and well-fought battle. I am just glad that the Obama team never got caught up in the race issue, although it was rearing its ugly head all throughout the campaign.

I know why most of minorities cannot get certain jobs, why over 21% of black males are in jail, why some want to end affirmative action, why mixed couples still get dirty looks, why some areas continue redlining, why college tuition has sky-rocketed, and why your whole life is based off of a credit report. I am not paranoid, I can see. It is just a shame that a lot of people don't see what is going on or challenge to change the system; not for the sake of hate but for love and justice.

A lot of children should be given a second chance for petty crimes. A lot more neighborhoods should be filled with after-school programs, camps, and affordable family counseling. More schools should have classes to educate teens on the importance of abstinence, credit, college, and saving for their future. More time should be invested in keeping people out of jail, rehabilitating those in jail, and helping those who went to jail get a fresh start when they come out so that they can live a productive and independent life. It is time for parents to push their children off to college, invest in their ideas, and stand behind them. We need to watch those movies as a reminder of where we don't ever want to see ourselves or anyone else again. We are African-Americans and our history is in these movies.

Even the bible is a huge history book of what was and what is to come. The bible tells us about African history. It is where civilization began. So we cannot afford to forget our history. We have to learn it for understanding and to teach our children so they can know who they are. The bible teaches us to forgive. Which means that we should not hate a particular race but embrace our differences.

We are not headless horsemen! We should not be running around aimlessly, without a mission. When we cover our eyes, close our ears, and shut our mouths we are killing our children. We have to stand behind them. And we have to teach them the right way to handle life's challenges.

My daughter was four years old when we walked into a particular restaurant in downtown Chicago.

She looked around at all of the people and then up at me and said, "Mommy, why aren't there any black people here? I don't want to eat here."

I told her that we were the black people there and we can eat wherever we want. The establishment never said black people could not eat there, however, my daughter felt uncomfortable like many of us in these situations. Some of us do not feel we belong or think it may be too expensive so we dismiss the idea of even going in.

Anyway, I told her we would bring black people there. And, we did over the years. Today, you can walk into that same restaurant and see people of all colors eating together. One time I reminded my daughter of what she said and then I whispered to her with a smile, "Look at that, we did it!"

See, a child sees and understands more than they are given credit for. Do not ever underestimate them. After all, they tackle the understanding of an entire language within their first two years of living. It takes an adult several years to even grasp some concept on a foreign language. If the wisdom of the old is not given to children, they grow up like a wild weed; angry and confused. It is our duty to guide them, invest in them, educate them, and instill rich morals in their minds. Trust me, the heart will find its' way through the rich soils of the mind. Our children have to know their past so they can stand up to a brave, new future. It is not our job to limit them but to help increase their understanding and teach them how to make things better.

Fried Green Tomatoes & Egg Plant Snack

3 green tomatoes
1 eggplant
1 egg
1½ cups of cornmeal
1/3 cup of olive oil
Seasonings: curry (optional), onion powder, garlic powder, salt, pepper

1. Whisk one egg with seasonings into a small boil
2. Heat Olive Oil in frying pan over medium heat
3. Slice green tomatoes and eggplant to desired thickness
4. Season cornmeal in separate bowl
5. Place each vegetable into egg mixture, then coat with cornmeal
6. Cook for 5 minutes on until brown on each side
7. Let drain on a paper towel

* Serve between two slices of bread with hot sauce or mustard

Servings: 4-6
Prep & Cook time: 15 minutes

<u>Suggested Scriptures</u>
Psalms 127:3
2 Corinthians 6:3
Proverbs 6:20
Titus 2:1-8
Job 32:6-22

Dear Lord,

Help me to be a great example for my children and the children I come in contact with. Help me to keep my word and be a stair step and not a stumbling block for them. Help me to teach them to make wise decisions, know when to take a stand, and understand when to back down. Lord, please do not allow me to be a hypocrite but a hero. Bless me with knowledge, understanding, compassion, wisdom, and love so that I can leave a legacy of your rich blessings to my family. Please keep close watch on my family and protect them and help us to be the best parents we can be. Thank you and I praise you in Jesus' name. Amen.

Meochia Nochi Thompson

About the 10th Piece
Don't Tell Them What You Know

You have to be careful about who you share your dreams with. There are some real dream killers out there. So you must use caution when you speak and protect yourself. My husband loves the saying, "Eagles don't fly with pigeons." In other words, if the company you keep isn't headed in the same direction you're going in, you need to either change course or change friends. Do whichever one is headed for higher ground.

Don't Tell Them What You Know

Tempers may flare and many may go
But please don't tell them what you know
They may understand what you are going through
But the best secrets kept are the ones with you
Times have changed but people hearts are the same
Avoiding any doubts and dodging blame
Fingers are pointed opposite of faces
All evidence points against but leaves no traces
Don't ask me why my head hangs low
The only hit that hurts is a truth blow
So, I'll mope for a while but in a minute I'll be okay
Don't tell me you understand what I am about to say
If you do then you know what I said was right
Lets just smile this away and rest for the night
By morning if my thoughts seize me give me a while to relax
It's just taking a little longer to get this load off my back
But whatever you do be careful to give what's on your mind
Because I tell you in due time
Tempers flare high and low and desires may come and go
But never, ever tell them what you know!

Beware of the Dream Killers

I was furious when I wrote this piece. Why does it seem like every time you confide in your man at some point it is thrown back in your face? I don't care how sincere they are at the time you tell them, it is going to come back out at some point. Now, he may not be bringing up your secrets to hurt you but it seems like it just stings coming out of his mouth.

Remember, even when you think men aren't paying attention to what you say, they are. Sometimes, it seems like they can be some of the nosiest and gossiping folks around. So be careful about what you tell them.

This same message applies to friendships. You must be careful about who you share your business with. People can be very envious and try to stop your success because of their own selfish ambitions. It's crazy. It is like telling a secret and expecting the person you told not to repeat it. Your name may have been changed but the story came out somewhere. Either they told or you told. Eventually, that story is going to get recycled. It is not a secret once it is released from your lips. Air is made to carry and transmit sound and whatever else. You shouldn't tell everything even if you think there is nothing to tell. I didn't say lie, I just said leave yourself some ammo.

Remember, new relationships are new starts, so leave that other baggage behind. If the information you are withholding is really going to affect your relationship, be sure this is the right person you want to share it with. Make sure this person sincerely wants to be with you and it is a mutual commitment. Also, be certain that he's understanding and trusting. You will know this by his actions. Also pray on it. If you do decide to tell him anything use discretion. Because, if you give all of you now, whatever will you have to give next? Nothing.

It is great when you have someone you can truly confide in. For instance, I know that I can trust my husband with my deepest secrets. We tell each other what is in our hearts and we keep it between us. Sometimes he fusses at me but I do know he has my best interest at heart.

Smothered Pork Chops In Stewed Tomato Sauce

1 green bell pepper
1 can of mushrooms or ½ pound of fresh mushrooms
1 can of whole or diced tomatoes
2 small cans of tomato sauce
1 tablespoon of minced garlic
4 pork chops
1 large, square baking pan
1 cup of water
Seasonings: salt, pepper, seasoning salt, garlic, onion powder
Aluminum foil

1.   Clean pork chops and place in baking pan
2.   Add huge square cuts of green onions and peppers
3.   Add tomato sauce, mushrooms, and diced tomatoes
4.   Add garlic and seasonings
5.   Cover with aluminum foil
6.   Place in oven for 1½ hours

*Turn meat every 30 minutes to keep it tender and moist

Servings: 4
Prep & Cook time: 2 hours

<u>Suggested Scriptures</u>
Proverbs 13:20
Genesis 37:5-8

Dear Lord,

Please protect my dreams and me. Let the people I share my dreams with be friends with my best interest in heart and mind. Protect me from my enemies and keep me from harm. Keep your hands around me, Lord. Help me to forgive others and forgive myself. Let me be a bigger and better person when the trials of life appear before me. Lord, make me as strong as the bamboo tree that my roots will be firmly planted and my leaves do not wilt in the hot sun. Help me to be a dream maker and not a dream killer, Lord. I'm ready to walk into the destiny you have planned for me. Guide my footsteps, guard my tongue, and bless my walk. Lord, I pray and ask all these things in Jesus' name. Amen.

About the 11th Piece
Woman in Waiting

It is hard to understand why couples fight so hard to stay together when they are just dating but when they get married they divorce for the simplest of reasons. The best thing a couple can do is respect each other's differences and try to move forward together. Remember, that was the person you couldn't get enough of before you said, "I do".

Woman In Waiting

I thought I loved him, until I became a woman...
The scent of his deodorant, I longed for cologne
His fast, short kisses, I wanted long, passionate, and lasting
His wise cracks, I wanted to be serious
His unreaching dreams, I longed for realization

She came, I grew--in mind
He, I left behind, but now-- I reach for him
He, who at first I thought I could not grasp
Is now raising his arms and extending
While I, who tried hard to let go, grip his wrists tighter
He has seen what it has to offer,
He, now, knows it is only temporary
I am forever, we are eternity
He, her, and I together

And so, I hold on
Now he is a man and I am still here
We have bonded, growing as one
On separate paths with the same destination
But growing and I wait, patiently
Now, I know I do.

Letting Go Is Never Easy

To wait is a powerful and important step in maturing emotionally. It could turn out good or blow up in your face but the choice is always yours to make. When I was younger, I left my daughter's father because I felt we weren't compatible. I wanted different things for myself. Back then I didn't understand that two matching cards don't necessarily mean a good pair. I learned that to get things going in a relationship you must have patience to wait, courage to endure, and God to keep it together. I learned to reach out and help instead of run away. I learned to give a relationship all I had to make it work.

I also learned that children make it hard to leave a relationship and that is where my daughter came in. When you bring a child into a relationship that has no marital commitment, it makes things more complicated. Now, you have to consider that child when you make crucial decisions regarding the other parent.

I learned that no one is born knowing everything and that I also make mistakes. I was asking a young man to behave like something he wasn't accustomed to and had ever even experienced. I wanted him to be a mature man, father, and husband without the ring.

When I realized I wasn't getting my way, I wanted to run away and complain. Instead of communicating what I wanted from him and allowing him to be a part of my decisions, I would get frustrated and shut down. He wasn't maturing fast enough for me. The child sped up our clocks, so I thought. I wanted him to be conservative. I wanted him to guide our family and know what he wanted. But, he was a baby just like me. He didn't even have all of the answers to his life yet.

Eventually, through wisdom and lots of trial and error, I learned to reach for him and our family. I learned to work with him. After we split up, we both realized that the world didn't have anything to offer. He really noticed that there was nothing out there for him. Just as I learned that it was hard to find a faithful, loving young man who wanted to be at home.

We didn't have to be carbon copies but we did have to possess an understanding of our selves and each other. Eventually, we got together again and tried to work things out. We became engaged but we broke up, again. We could not keep sending our child through our harsh growing pains. I think our experience helped us in our own marriages, later. It also became a great teaching tool for my daughter.

The lesson from these experiences is to let God be the focus and to hold fast and wait until marriage before giving yourself to a man. Also make sure you know what you really want out of life and learn to communicate your feelings effectively before you become committed to someone. I told my daughter that I would never want my grandchildren to experience what she had to if they do not have to. But, it all starts with God and self-control.

This poem went from questioning love to knowing love.

Beefy Stir Fry

1½ pounds of beef strips (shrimp and chicken optional)
1 large green pepper
1 large onion
1 can of mushrooms or 6 fresh mushrooms sliced
1 tablespoon of minced garlic
2 ½ cups of rice
Seasoning: onion powder, garlic powder, pepper, seasoning salt, soy sauce (optional)
2 tablespoons of olive oil
Wok or deep Frying Pan

1. Cut meat into thin strips
2. Cut onion, green pepper into medium pieces
3. Add oil to wok over high heat
4. Add beef and seasonings and cook until brown throughout
5. Add all the vegetables
6. Cook for about 15 minutes, stirring constantly
7. The mixture should produce a small, thick gravy add a little water to produce more
8. Cook rice
9. Place rice in bowls and top with stir-fry

Servings: 4-6
Prep & Cook time: 30 minutes

Suggested Scriptures
1 Peter 3:1,7
Titus 2:4
1 Corinthians 7:3, 10, 32-35 and 39
Proverbs 12:4,19:3

Dear Lord,

If my mate and I are living outside of your will please help us to get on track and in line with you. Put marriage into our future so that our family may be blessed by living according to your word, Father. Help my husband and I to respect each other by putting your reasons before our own. Lord, help us to make it through the struggles and toils of our relationship by remembering what is truly important. Bless us with staying power, Lord because we know that Satan hates marriage and will try anything to pull us apart. Please do not allow our hearts to become hardened against each other or allow us to give in to lust and temptation. Lord, bless every relationship we come into contact with. Bless our families and our children. Let us seek you as our glorious head, Lord. Help me to submit to my husband as he submits to you. Lord, let us lean not to our own understanding but seek your knowledge and wisdom. Thank you for your love and your mercy. Thank you for the gift of life. Thank you for your grace. Thank you for caring for my family and I when we could not care enough for ourselves. Thank you for blessing and protecting us when we were clearly outside of your will. Oh Lord, your grace is sufficient. Thank you, Almighty God for loving me. I pray and give thanks in Jesus' name. Amen.

About the 12th Piece
Him, Her and I

Since when did "Man-sharing" become okay? A lot of women lose a lot of their years sleeping with someone else's man. Some do it because it seems safe, they think he really loves them or they can't move on without him. Whatever the reason, there is no justification for it. True relationships are built on trust and you simply can't trust someone who is living a lie. So get some confidence, patience, and faith in God. He will send you a man of your own.

Him, Her and I

i used to love him
the scent of his cologne
his passionate kisses
his warm and knowledgeable conversations
he was wonderful
but
she wouldn't let him go
and i couldn't have him
he wouldn't let me go
i asked him
not really wanting an answer
he never said yes
so
i'm trapped forever
because if she releases
i may be freed and want to be
he's still handsome, smart, and good to me
but i wonder
without her is he good for me?

The Other Woman

Being the other woman seems fun at first because there isn't a real commitment. But the first woman always gets the last laugh. A real woman knows how to walk away quietly in defeat. What you'll find is that most of the time that man is only good for an affair and actually sucks in a real relationship. So let go of somebody else's man and get your own.

That greener grass will get you every time if you are not careful. Sometimes you do not realize how people can dump such treasures until you take it home and have to trash it yourself. I was in love with someone else's love. I thought I wanted him so bad at first. But love is always so good when it is fresh. After a while I began to notice things that even I couldn't bare about him. I began to renegotiate the risks of him leaving her and ending up with me. I decided I liked him best when he was someone else's burden.

See, I was selling myself short by giving him the best of both worlds. At the time, I thought the sex was great. I soon learned that my dignity was even greater. I also realized that I was hurting myself and another sister, who may have had no clue as to what her man was up to. I just knew that I didn't want to be the one getting hurt in the end, so this lifestyle was safe for my own heart's protection. But, everything is good when you are just borrowing it and you don't have to maintain it. The best thing was to let him go.

Also, do not ever fall victim to the "what ifs". That is the lesson I had to learn when I tried to rekindle a relationship with this same guy when we both were single. I found out that some things are better left to wonder about than to actually know. Sometimes the past has to be left right where it is. Dreams are so much better than reality because they allow justice to be served and you get predictable endings. On the other hand, reality can be harsh and regretful. Things between us never worked out because he was still playing the same old games. In fact, when he finally felt like he was done being a player and wanted to start another relationship with me, I didn't even consider it! I had to move on with my life. I knew I had to get right. He had his own journey to deal with.

So sisters let go of lying men and do not become a home wrecker. Why would you continue on with someone that is deceitful? And, how can you expect a man to trust you if you are being deceitful? Ask yourself if you would really want her man if he were single? If he was so good and in love with you, why is he still laying with her? That "it's the children" excuse is dead. Then ask yourself, why is he cheating on his family? Don't you deserve a man of your own? Don't you deserve a husband? If he tricked her, he doesn't really care about tricking you. And what about your life? You do not want the man you fall in love with to lie to you, do you?

We all make mistakes. Nobody is perfect, except Jesus. So, this bad relationship doesn't mean the end for you. You can fully recover. Do not punish yourself. You can have a happy marriage or relationship of your own. Don't let your past hunt you. Clean it up by repenting and asking God for forgiveness and looking forward to a greater future with an honest man of your own.

I had to let go of my past and give my future to God. I learned to trust Him because He is faithful. You have to do the same for yourself. Now, I could have not asked for a better husband. He is honest and faithful to God and me. I don't run behind him checking to see if he is cheating on me. I also don't beat myself up over my past life. I just give my testimony as a pearl of wisdom to someone else who is struggling with a bogus relationship like I was.

Pig In The Blanket with Cabbage and Beef

1 ½ pound of ground beef
1 large onion
2 16-ounce cans of tomato sauce
1 8-ounce can of tomato paste
1 cup of rice
1 cabbage (large and very green)
8 cups of water
Seasonings: salt, pepper, onion powder

1. Parboil cabbage for 15 min. to soften some layers of leaves
2. Peel leaves
3. Cook rice
4. Mix rice, tomato paste, and seasonings into ground beef
5. Roll beef mixture into medium-sized balls and place inside cabbage leaf and roll until beef is completely wrapped (this usually only requires one leaf)
6. Now place cabbage ball into a large pot
7. Make sure the cabbage is place downwards in the pot so it won't come loose while cooking
8. Repeat
9. Cut up leftover cabbage over the mixture
10. Chop onions into large pieces and place in pot
11. Add tomato paste and water
12. Season cabbage and cook on medium for an hour
13. Turn fire down if over boiling occurs
14. Make sure beef is cooked thoroughly

*Serve with cornbread

Servings: 4-6
Prep & Cook time: 1½ hours

<u>Suggested Scriptures</u>
Titus 2:11-14
2 Corinthians 7:9-11

Dear Lord,

Forgive me for my sins of lust and perversion. Forgive me for committing idolatry, adultery, and fornication because these things are not of you, Lord. Help me to become stronger and resilient. Help me to resist temptation. I know that I am weak but I must trust that you will get me through any and all of my hard times. Lord, I don't feel good about what I do when I am disobedient to you but it is hard to walk away sometimes. Lord, please fill the empty gaps and voids in my life that cause me to make these lonely decisions. I am so helpless without you, Lord. I recognize that my strength comes from you. I do not want to live in this prison of hopelessness and despair that I have been living in. I do desire to be independent and break free of these sins of imprisonment. I would like a loving and trusting relationship of my own. I do want to be released from the hate, anger, and trust issues that I have been bound by. Reach for me, Lord. Pull me out of this deep pit I have dug for myself. Clean me up and teach me how to walk upright in your glory. Help me, Lord. I need you. I know I am weak but you said where I am weak you are strong. You said, "My yoke is easy". Lord, you said you came that I may have life and have it more abundantly. Lord, keep your hands on me. Pull me out. Let my enemies and friends see how much you love me and let them adore how much you have changed my life. Lord, I am asking you to help me have a change of mind and heart. I am inviting you into my life, Lord. My soul yearns to do what is right in your eyes. Please don't let my flesh condemn me, Lord. I pray and ask for your favor in Jesus' name. Amen.

About the 13th Piece
Press On

So many people grow up in dysfunctional families and relationships. Not everyone is fortunate to have a background they are very proud of. However, from these circumstances come great testimonies. No matter our situation, we must keep the faith and keep moving. We must learn to let go and let God. We spend too much time worrying about things that are beyond our control. Just give God the wheel and relax. No matter what roadblocks you face in life keep the faith and keep going. Always press onward.

Press On

You just
Press on my sister
Press on my sister
Press on my sister
Press on

At times when I am faced with adversities
Something in my backbone causes me to stand straight up
Something in feet just causes me to walk
Something in my knees just makes my legs lock in an upright
position and I just press on
Something in my hips causes me to sway that way
With that confident stride that makes my neck hide
The sorrow as my head tilts upward for better tomorrows
And then and then
My arms begin to sway like weeping willows in the wind with
golden hands attached
Snatching at opportunities and grabbing whatever I choose
My shoulders are strong and sharp never sagging
As my nipples perk up at the constant nagging of success
In my ear making my back get chills as I press on
My neck is like a man; support for the heavy head
It carries it like a treasure
That beautiful skin
That brilliant color
That strong hair
Those hopeful eyes
That spiritual mind
That pumps that faithful heart
Those dynamic ears
That observant nose
That tilted forehead
That knows where it's about to go
As I press on
Excuse me for stepping on your shoes
It seems I haven't quite grown into mine yet

And I keep stumbling all over the place
But I feel myself growing, always knowing
In the forefront of this upside-down pyramid of colors
I stand as Queen
I am not bothered
I will not be sidetracked
I am following that glow before me
That always seems to go every time I get distracted
Now shoo!
Fly away as I continue on my journey into my destiny–
Not yours
You'll have to wait until I grow some more as I press on
Oh! What is this? My shoes aren't slipping any more
In fact, they seem a bit tiny
I think I might need a new pair
That is alright, right?
Can I borrow those?
Better yet let me buy my own because I am doing it now
How about you?
Now reach up there and get those down for me
Wow! You're growing too
You need more shoes!
Now we seem to be the perfect fit
Now listen to me as we both sit
I don't want this reality check to be too hard of a hit
But find some business to tend to like you
Until I finish what for me was meant
Or I will just press on.

Keep On Pushing Forward

This poem is all about putting the past behind you and removing any obstacles that come your way. It's about keeping your head up when the stakes are against you. It's about taking care of you.

I was at a low point in my life. Everything seemed to be coming down on me at once. My roommate wasn't paying rent, my daughter didn't have any Christmas gifts, and I didn't have a job. The unemployment checks had ceased. And you know how they are. After your first notification, they don't warn or remind you about your cut off date…the checks just stop coming. I hit a dead end.

My ex-boyfriend and I had rekindled our relationship exactly where we left off; him broke and still struggling to get his business off the ground. I loved him so much and hated myself for being so impatient. And, I really couldn't stand time because it was and is non-biased; it does not wait for anyone. My guy wasn't growing up fast enough for me. It seems like I had a pattern of these types of guys in my life. I felt like he was holding me back and pulling me down. I wanted him to give me some direction, instead we were arguing about which way to go. I was so lost. How could I lead him somewhere when I wasn't really sure as to where I was going? I needed Jesus more than ever. We needed Jesus.

Something inside of me was bursting to get out. Something in my spirit had an appointment with life and my own procrastinating ways was holding it back. My soul would not let my eyes sleep or my heart get weary and my mind was constantly racing. I needed to get on with my life. I knew God had something for me and I had to find it.

I remember sitting at the kitchen table with my head down and thinking about how bad my problems were. Then I just started to pray. I said, "God, here we go again, I need your help!" I bowed my head one more time. And just like that I began to jump and shout as the melody began to press out of my mouth, "Press on my sister, press on. Press on my sister, press on!"

This poem is for all the sisters who have things in their lives that are holding them back to press on. This poem is an anthem for freedom! The same day I wrote it, I recorded my first musical track, Press On My Sister!

We let so many things get in our way and distract us from what God has for us. Sometimes you just have to say no, goodbye, that's okay, maybe next time, or I can't do it right now. You have to make yourself a priority in your life. Once you begin putting you first, people will begin to look at you in a different light and respect you more.

In this life, you are responsible for your own life. When you die, God is going to hold you accountable for your sins and not anyone else. So, you have to decide who is more important when you go to answer for yourself. In the end, God will definitely show you it is you and Him. So make the right decisions for you and put everything else to the side. Let the baggage go, look ahead to your future, and press on with life. Grow into your shoes and walk into your destiny!

The next recipe will give your tongue a musical treat of tropical flavoring for your thirsty taste buds.

Pow-Wow Punch

1-2 packages of favorite powdered fruit drink
½ cup of sugar
1 can of pineapple chunks
Extra Add-ins:
grapes
cherries
mandarin orange slices
peaches
fruit cocktail
ice

1. Mix all the fruit into a pitcher; including pineapple juice
2. Pour in drink mix and stir
3. Add sugar as needed
4. Chill for at least an hour or add ice for instant servings
5. Finally, you have a ready to serve a delicious drink that tastes wonderful

Servings: 4+
Prep & Cook time: 10 minutes

Suggested Scriptures
Philippians 3:12-16
Galatians 5:1,7 and 6:9
Hebrews 12:1-3,11-13

Dear Lord,

In this world of uncertainty, perversion, and violence give me the strength to press on, Lord. Help me to never lose sight of you and your ways. Lord, keep my family protected, heavily guarded, and equipped with your weapons of spiritual warfare. Lord, thank you for blessing me with the gift of faith and cleansing me of the spirit of fear because fear is not from you! Thank you for giving me faith, courage, and love. Thank you for forgiving, Lord. Keep your hands on me, your eyes on me, and your light on me. Lord, continue to bless me with your selfless love. Keep pushing me towards my destiny, pulling me in your direction, and encouraging me to press on. In Jesus' name I pray, Amen!

About the 14th Piece
Awaken

When was the last time you felt inspired? Or felt a burning desire to push forward? You can get so caught up in your past situations that you begin to close up, not wanting to burden anyone else with your problems. But if and when someone does come into your life to help you lift the baggage from the past off your shoulders don't reject them. It can be a big relief. Don't carry that dead weight, get it off your chest, and give it to God. Wake up and renew yourself in the Lord, it's a brand new day!

Awaken

You wake me
Putting breath into my empty mouth
And feeding my thirsty passion
You shake calmness
And stir madness into my innocent dreams
My love is screaming for your desire
Hoping, wanting, and praying that you will reach for me
Binding me to your soulful eyes
Never releasing me to reality again.

Hoping For Love

The world is a tough place to live in, especially when you are facing it alone. You'd think with all of your independence and freedom that you wouldn't yearn for a relationship but you do. At the end of the day, we all crave it.

You can have the car, career, and home of your dreams but without someone to share it with, it means nothing. Don't even try the pet thing. Pets cannot talk back and they cannot comprehend your dreams or help solve your problems. But I guess they are good listeners.

My young child was a good listener, too but I am not quite sure she was fully paying attention to everything I said or even interested for that matter. I needed companionship. I needed to love and be loved. There was a time in my life when I felt that I did my best work when I was alone. No matter how good the work was, however, it still felt like something was empty inside me. I needed to share my happiness with someone else.

I discovered I needed someone who could support my endeavors and see them as a positive and not be intimidated. In other words, the problem was not with me being in a relationship, it was the men I was choosing to be in a relationship with. Isn't that what we are here for, love recycling…companionship…each other?

I wrote this poem after I met my husband. He inspired me. He made me want to pursue my dreams of becoming a great writer. He awakened all the gifts that God stored up in me. I wanted to do more than I was doing. He was sharpening me, bending me, and pushing me to my limit. He awakened hope in my spirit and inspired me to be my best. Awaken is a poem of passion directed at the heart and not the body.

Banana Pudding In the Mix

7 bananas
1 box of banana pudding
1 box of vanilla wafers
1 small package of whip cream (optional)
1 cup of cherries (optional)
2 tablespoons of cinnamon
Round casserole dish

1. Mix pudding
2. Cut bananas into thin slices
3. Layer in order of cookies, pudding, and bananas
4. On final layer add whip cream topping and cherries
5. Cover and refrigerate for about 2 hours

*For traditional pudding don't add whip cream or cherries

Servings: 6+
Prep & Cook time: 2½ hours

<u>Suggested Scriptures</u>
Ephesians 4:1-2, 5:19
Galatians 6:1-2

Dear Lord,

Thank you for my passion and gifts, Lord. Thank you for keeping me on the right track by helping me to stay focused. Lord, my desire is not to be alone. Please help me to recognize that being with you is never being alone. Lord, send sincere hearted people my way who will help strengthen me in my time of weakness. I need people in my life that will encourage, uplift, and carry me when I am too weak to move forward. Lord, keep stirring up the passion in my heart to fulfill the destiny you have set before me with the many gifts you have entrusted to me. Lord, I don't ever want to feel lonely or misplaced again. You said your burden is light and your yolk is easy. Lord, carry me and mine. Help me to unleash these problems and worries I have been carrying. I know now that they aren't anything but distractions designed to keep me away from my true calling. Lord, thank you for listening and thank you for loving me. Lord, I know there is someone out there that desires the same things that I desire. Someone who wants a friend they can love and trust just as much as I do. Lord, bring us together so that we can keep each other strong and encouraged. I pray and ask these things in Jesus' name. Amen.

Meochia Nochi Thompson

About the 15th Piece
To Kiss A King

Wisdom is the only way a woman learns exactly what a man wants and needs. The only ways to gain wisdom is to listen and learn. Too many times young women are quick to think they know all the answers. Eventually, we waste a lot of time "casting our pearls before swine" and giving too much of ourselves too soon. It is not appreciated and our feelings get hurt. Learn to slow down and say "no", trust God, be patient, and pray for the wisdom and knowledge you need in life. Sex was never a way to a man's heart; it is only the quickest way to his bed. If you want to keep someone happy, learn to make yourself happy first.

To Kiss A King

You start off slowly caressing his head in the bed
Making love to his mind with your lips resting gently upon his
forehead

You, then, glide your lips slowly from one temple to the next to
ease his stress and slow his pain
And to remind him that by the end of the night you'll make him
scream your name

You next, rush to his eyes giving them both equal attention and
kissing them long and deep
Letting him know when you first looked into his, your heart was
his for keeps

Then, starting between his brows you lick from the top to the very
end of his strong nose, adding an extra kiss at the tip, to show you
sense his trial and will stay through his tribulation
Let him breathe your natural scent and long for your sweet
infatuation

Next, you give long kisses to each of the textured cheeks on his
chiseled face then you softly rub you palms across them and look
into his eyes and then place your cheeks upon his and move away
You are now showing him your love is forever because forever
doesn't fade

Slide gradually down towards his thick, sweet lips like warm, slow
molasses
I guarantee he will get chills like a baby with heat rashes

You see, Kings are strong men so you have to get them to bend but
only to you
So, this final kiss is very important, take notes if you have to...

You lick the middle tip of his top lip, then part them both with your tongue and suck on the inside, then the bottom then both together

Yeah, girl, I promise you this is the most important kiss ever

You are tasting his words, loving his voice, teasing his tone and awakening his moan...
You are inviting him and enlightening him and playing temptation with his groans

To kiss a King, you don't have to be an excellent lover but you do have to know how to love
You have to assure your man he's the only one you even think of

You have to empty your mind and forget your problems for the moment and be in complete unison with him
You have to drink him, sleep him, and love him on the whim

You have to touch his head, kiss his ears, lick his neck, and rub his back...
And when he goes to do the same for you say, "Stop it baby...just relax."

You have to grab his shoulders, massage his neck, and straddle his waist
Wear your silk, wear your satin, wear your leather, or wear your lace

You have to know when to be silent and when to speak
When to stand strong and how to be weak

When to be careless and how to admit your wrong
Know when it's time to get back quick or stay away long...

When he simply wants to talk and when to make love
When to walk away and when to give a hug

Where he needs to be kissed and what he needs more of
When to voice your opinion and when you've said enough

To kiss a king, you have to be willing to teach and be taught
You have to chase and be willing to get caught

Know a lot but not too much
Surrender to his strength and crumble at his touch

You have to tell him you love him and tell him he's been missed
Love his inner beauty and seal it all with a kiss…

What Separates the Woman From the Girl?

Young ladies tend to think that loving a man has to do with sex. They get sore advice from other girls, magazines, the internet, TV, and radio telling them that's all men want. Sex, sex, and more sex! Sorry ladies, that isn't what it is all about. True, men do love sex but why? They love it because it makes them feel powerful, strong, and in control (even if they aren't). It makes them equal to any other man. This is the only time that his wealth isn't really measured. This is a time when he is fully giving himself to you. He is imparting his spirit into you. That is why it is important to only lay with your husband.

No matter how big and bad we think we are; it is hard to shake a man. They leave a part of themselves behind when they lay with us; it doesn't leave the bedroom with them. Since we are made to carry, we take all of his emotions, his pains, and his gains into our bodies. We allow him to release all that into us. Here's a wake up call: with or without protection, he is still entering into your sacred place.

Men desire to be loved and appreciated. He likes hearing how handsome he is, how helpful he is, how smart, and strong he is. Just as much as we like to hear that we are supportive, beautiful, pretty, smart, and strong. If you cannot say anything nice about your man, you need to reevaluate the choice you made or find out why he isn't doing anything you can compliment him on.

Sometimes it isn't him that is the problem. Sometimes we are just never satisfied or set standards we couldn't even reach as a man. Notice the poem calls him what he is--a "King". He was made to rule over. We should be building him up, not tearing him down. We should be appreciating him for all that he does, big or small. He needs that encouragement like a simple kiss of love.

I read this poem to so many married couples and they fell in love with it. Some wives have called me and said they followed it step by step and even memorized it! I am thrilled. I wrote this poem because I hear so many men talking about how women don't appreciate them or only care about what they can get out of the relationship. This poem is meant as a guide and wake up call to all those sisters who may have thought they knew what was best. This is the official recipe to kissing a King. By the way, the ability to learn and apply is one of the many things that separate a woman from a girl.

Please learn how to be a loving wife to your husband and seek helpful advice from other women in loving relationships. I remember cringing every time my mother said that it makes a man feel important when they know they can teach you something. She said even if you do know the answer you should just let him say it sometimes. Well, I felt like that would be degrading myself just to make some insecure man feel very important. Well, she was right and it works. I know my husband is very secure and super confident. When I tried the wise way of letting him show me the way, it seemed to make him relax a little and I think his chest even grew some. Although I was laughing to myself about it, I can tell you that it got me way further with him than I was before.

What I have learned through experience is that men are natural problem solvers. If you don't have any problems or things they can fix, you don't need them and therefore you don't present any type of challenge. Sure they will admire your wit and your smarts but they want to know that they can add something of value to you. This does not mean you should act like a bimbo. It just means that you have to let him win sometimes. It feels good after you do it a couple of times. You'll even find yourself getting a kick out of the fact that he really thinks he knows it all. We all know that women are smarter. It just takes them a little bit longer to figure it out. Kiss, kiss!

Magnificent Mac

8 ounces of Provolone Cheese
16 ounces of shredded mild cheddar cheese
16 ounces of shredded sharp cheddar cheese
8 ounces of shredded mozzarella cheese
8 ounces of Swiss cheese
8 ounces of American cheese
1 stick of margarine
6 eggs
3 cups of milk
Seasonings: salt, pepper, paprika (optional)
1 box of macaroni
Large Aluminum Baking Pan

1. Preheat oven to 400°.
2. Boil water and cook macaroni
3. Add eggs, salt, and pepper to a large bowl and whisk lightly
4. Mix all cheeses together
5. Place macaroni in large aluminum baking pan and add milk, cheeses, eggs, and butter
6. Cover with wax paper and aluminum foil
7. Place mixture in oven for 1 hour until cheese melts
8. Remove covering and cook for 30 minutes to brown top
9. Remove from oven and lightly sprinkle top with paprika

*Serve with salad and/or garlic bread

Servings: 6+
Prep & Cook time: 1½ hours

<u>Suggested Scriptures</u>
1 Corinthians 13
Song of Songs 1-8
Titus 2:3-5
1 Peter 3:1-6

Dear Lord,

Let the people call me blessed by the wonderful fruit that I bear. Let words of kindness and encouragement come from my mouth. Let me see myself with as much value as you do for your lost sheep. Help me to abstain from things that are not of you, Lord. Yes, the flesh is weak, Lord but a spirit that is well vested and rooted in you can conquer the flesh just as you have conquered death. Lord, keep your hands on me and help me to be a woman of virtue, beauty, grace, and honor. Let me give off a spirit of love and compassion for my family, and especially my husband. Let me speak words of kindness to him. Keep him seeking your face and thanking you for such a lovely bride. Lord, protect me from the wolves in sheep clothing so that I may not cast my pearls amongst swine. Help me to be patient and wait on you. Help me to love myself by seeing you in myself and respecting my temple. I know that you have good plans for me, Lord, and I pray that I am obedient and strong enough to carry them out. I love you Almighty, marvelous, and wonderful God of mystery and splendor. Thank you for loving me more than I can ever love myself and providing all of my wants and needs. I pray all these things in Jesus name, Amen.

About the 16th Piece
Lines

Words...the whole world began with just words; God's word. He said it and so it came to past. That alone, tells us how very important they are. People live and die based off of them. Nowadays, technology makes it so easy for us to communicate with people from all parts of the earth. The problem is that it is becoming more difficult to decipher the truth from a lie. In the past, you could look someone in the eyes and possibly notice deception. Nowadays, people have become cleverer about hiding the truth.

Lines

Are these some of the lines you use to get your page filled?
Some of the lines you use to make a sister feel
Like she has reached the last of her line
And you are the beginning
Leaving other prospects in the dust
And trails of broken hearts with no endings?

Are these some of the lines you drop in seas of women for bate?
Hoping their bellies will get filled off of the words they ate?

Are these some of the lines that leave angels touched?
Or pieces of the little things that ladies love so much?

Are these some of the lines you hope will woo thee?
Or do you intend on coming a little bit better to impress a sista like
me?

Lines can come long, strong, straight, narrow or thick
But to catch traces of thin air you have to be pretty quick.

You have to think on your feet, move fast, stay steady
And step up to the plate only if you're ready.

Because no lines live here just ones to phone cords
Ones that I plug into when I get bored
Ones that only respond if I chose to plug them in
Ones that get done once the phone gets hung.

Don't come bringing no lines in here
Those colorful thoughts you released won't sell
I've been known for cutting tones
And giving brothers who speak too well, hell.

Don't Get Full Off Empty Words

Have you ever met someone that you just knew was up to no good? He was handsome, said everything you needed to hear, and had the right walk and talk…I mean he was just so right. But somewhere in the back of your mind didn't you know that he was wrong? You listened to his garbage and you devoured it. Something in the pit of your stomach told you he wasn't right. You had a nagging sensation throughout your body that said this guy is a liar. Well, when you don't take heed to your own warnings and that relationship terminates, you get very angry. So, you end up snapping on the next guy who comes around and attempts to play that same tired line game with you. Why? You do it because you have heard it all before. That's wisdom and experience, baby! The key is not to get angry but learn to recognize game, and not fall for it, again.

If you know someone is no good for you or feeding you lies, get him out of your life. The tongue has the power of life and death in it. It is a flesh and spirit killer. You take in all of its poisons and sooner or later it just kills you. On the other hand, if you eat of its sweet and good fruits, it can heal you, as well. But no lie has ever made anyone's life better. The truth may sting for a while but at least you know what is really going on, and can make a conscious decision based on what's right. That is why the saying goes, if you don't stand up for something, you will fall for anything. Stand up for yourself. Don't believe the lies. Do not allow a liar into your life. The truth hurts but it does set you free. Trust your gut instinct. Trust God enough to know that he will put people in your life who don't mean you any harm. People who really want to help you and will love you the way you want and need to be.

Tempting Lemon Peppered Tilapia

4 pieces of tilapia
2 tablespoon of fresh or minced garlic
1 tablespoon of ground pepper
1 tablespoon of lemon pepper
¾ cups of lemon juice or one fresh lemon
1 tablespoon of butter cut into four thin pieces
Large baking pan

1. Preheat oven to 350°
2. Wash thawed fish and place on baking pan
3. Lightly sprinkle garlic, pepper, and lemon juice on top of fish
4. Add slices of butter to top of each piece
5. Cover and bake for 20 minutes

*Do not overcook or the fish will dry out
*Serve with brown rice and steamed asparagus, mash potatoes, and corn or salad

Servings: 4
Prep & Cook time: 25 minutes

<u>Suggested Scriptures</u>
Ephesians 5:6
Ephesians 4:22
Proverbs 18:1-7, 20-22
Proverbs 17:4, 19:1

Dear Lord,

Guard my ears and bless my tongue. Lord, strengthen my eyes, filter my ears, and shield my mind from corrupt information that tries to break through. Bless me with the spirit of discernment so that I may see my enemies when they come through dressed as innocent friends who really come to do me harm and speak words of hatred, dismay, and division. Strengthen my prayer life so that I learn to communicate better with you and I can call on you in my times of darkness. Lord, hold liars accountable and set the truth free. Lord, I thank you, love you, and praise you for your loving ears and kind words of life, mercy, and justice in Jesus' name. Amen.

About the 17th Piece
The Best Thing

Learning to accept the truth is a natural part of growing up. It is a shame to go through life, knowingly falling into deception. We begin caring about some other person more than ourselves, lusting after them, and placing them on a pedestal. It's modern day idolatry. We shouldn't put anything before the love of God. Most of us end up single longer than we want to because we allow ourselves to get into dysfunctional relationships for our own selfish desires. In the end, however, our misguided schemes backfire and leave us empty. I can still hear my momma saying, "I told you so."

The Best Thing

The best thing I've ever done is erased his number from my book
The hardest thing I could have ever done, you should have seen
how long it took

He wasn't no good for me, although he made me weak in the knees
I threw my morals out the door just to make sure he was pleased
He drove a red convertible which plates should have read
"Trouble"
I mean he could call me at 5 a.m. and I'd be there on the double
He had smooth caramel skin and a face that was covered with
freckles
With curly blond and light brown colored hair and an attitude like
Heckle and Jeckle
He had a body that was very defined
And in the dictionary under "fine"
This boy was so cold that he started sending me out of my mind

He didn't want anyone else to have me, yet he didn't want me for
himself
I was the greatest girl he could've ever had and the biggest fool he
ever kept
Thought it was cool to let him hang out with his friends drinking
gin
I was too afraid to tell him no or let him know what I was thinking
I guess if I didn't give a care I could handle it better than I am
But he really had me caught up and put my heart in a jam

He was so passionate when another man was around
But when we talked one on one he would never mutter a sound
(Except "Give it to me baby!")
He didn't make good love and reminded me constantly of what he
wouldn't do
And if you looked down at his shoes you'd tell me I was a plum
fool
He had me going--one look and I was pulling em' down
I don't know about love taps but the boy sure knew how to pound

And it ain't like he took care of me, gave me money or took me to dinner
I couldn't hear my mama laughing at me now saying, "Girl you really picked a fine winner!"

Now I ain't saying he was broke, he just didn't have no money or time for me
And although his personality wasn't all that, I liked him because he was so funny
Yeah, he loved to show me off but he never wanted to be seen
He was so trifling but he sure took the breath out of me!

Now, you asked if I had learned a lesson or if I would do it all again?
Well, you need to just mind your business cause I never asked for your opinion.

If the Shoe Don't Fit, He Ain't the Right Prince

You know, sometimes you gotta get through to your girls in a language they can understand. Almost all women either understand shopping language or shoe language. It all adds up to money but that is another issue. If the shoe does not fit, do not try to force it on your foot. It causes way too much pain and ugliness in the long run.

Well, I was head over heels infatuated with a man that absolutely got on my nerves. I had never fully experienced lust until I met him. He was gorgeous and he knew it. I remember hearing my mother talk about never falling for a man that thinks he looks better than you. But I never expected that to happen to me. I found myself accepting behavior I would have never put up with before. I was doing things I only saw crazy girls do like showing up at his house uninvited, arguing with him in public over another woman, and visiting him at odd times of the night wherever he chose to meet. It was crazy. I had to get a grip. I had to get back to normal. I was completely out of control. It finally came to a point where I had to stop lying to myself and falling for his lies.

How could I be faithful to someone or expect them to be faithful to me when my own intentions were not pure? Also, I was not being faithful to God. It can be a drag when you start really looking at the truth of the matter. After a while, he became so gross to me. He was no longer the pretty boy I thought of him as in the beginning. I even noticed that the more I pulled away from him, the more he drew closer to me because he wasn't used to rejection. It was a game I would have been playing the rest of my life with him.

Lust is not the only addiction that we get caught up in. It could be drugs, food, pornography, the need for acceptance by family or friends, gossip, money, shopping or anything else we place above God. You may not see it that way at first but think about it. If you find yourself feeling like something else is controlling you because you cannot be without it, you are coveting or you are committing a form of idolatry. The only one you should have no desire to be without is our Lord and Savior, Jesus Christ. God is all you need to survive and everything else is secondary.

We must set standards, boundaries, morals, and rules. We must live by them, also. The moment that a woman decides to take herself off of her pedestal, a man will view her differently. Follow God, set his standard, and move forward. It may seem to take long but it will be well worth the wait because you won't go wrong. Everything will not always be perfect; God guaranteed that but he did promise that if we keep His word, we will be rewarded, and he will give us the victory. So, don't get caught up in the fight because our battles are already won. Wait for God to bless you with the right one. If you're wondering, "How will I know?" All I can say is trust me, you will know.

Open-faced Crispy Baked Wings

2 pounds of chicken wings
Seasonings: salt, pepper, seasoning salt, garlic powder, onion powder, lemon pepper
Olive oil spray
Cookie sheet

1. Preheat oven to 450°
2. Place thawed chicken wings in sink and wash thoroughly
3. Sparingly sprinkle with all seasonings & spray lightly with olive oil (optional-adds extra crispiness)
4. Do not fold wings
5. Place wings on cookie sheet sprayed with olive oil
6. Place in oven and cook for 30 minutes
7. Turn wings over on tips and cook for additional 45 minutes until golden brown and crispy

*Serve with fried potatoes or salad

Servings: 4-6
Prep & Cook time: 1½ hours

<u>Suggested Scriptures</u>
Romans 7:7-21, 8:5-9
Matthew 7:6
1 Corinthians 6:12-20, 15:33
Colossians 3:5-10
James 4:17
1 John 5:21
Proverbs 12:15

Dear Lord,

Please forgive me for getting into relationships that go against your word. Forgive me for committing idolatry by worshiping anyone or thing other than you. Forgive me for putting my own selfish wants and needs before yours. Forgive me for my sins of lust, envy, adultery, selfishness, and greed. Forgive me for willingly putting myself into dysfunctional relationships. Help me to keep my attention focused on you and what is good in your eyes. Give me the strength to not fall into temptation. Please deliver me from evil. My desire is to do what is good in your eyes, Lord. I want to live right and do right but it seems like evil is waiting at my doorsteps and following close behind me. Lord, please protect me and help me gain the upper hand on my weaknesses. Lord, I repent of every sin of that I committed against you and I beg for your forgiveness and grace. I pray and ask that you continue to keep your hands on me, guiding me onto the path of righteousness. I pray in Jesus' name. Amen.

About the 18th Piece
Pruned to Bloom

The hardest criticism is self-criticism. That means looking at yourself and honestly accessing what you see. Sometimes we get into "saint mode". That is when we feel like we can do no wrong. We feel that as long as we aren't killing, lying, cheating, or stealing we are pretty good folks. Well, there are some slumps that we can fall prey to especially if they aren't checked. So guard your eyes, ears, mind, mouth, and heart. And, always seek God in everything you do.

Pruned to Bloom

FIVE BEAUTIFUL SEEDS

Before I begin to tell you my story or the process I was in
I'll let you peek inside my social life into the lives of my five
friends.
Now when I started my journey everyone seemed so fine.
In fact, the only situation that appeared messed up was mine.
Now I didn't try to hide my problems or my circumstance,
I just learned to let go and let God and not depend on man.
But enough about me- lets explore the soil's darkness to see what
the dirt hides:
Five seeds waiting to birth the beautiful flowers inside.
Now one of these scenarios may be yours or may be not
The point is your life will run smoother when you realize God is
all you got.
He creates your humble circumstance to bring you closer to His
voice
Because you'll never hear His call if you're constantly surrounded
by noise.
So don't be discouraged by your current situation in fear of
meeting your doom.
God picks us apart, first starting with our hearts because we are
pruned to bloom!

FIRST SEED- DISMISS LOW SELF-ESTEEM

My first friend was so messed up; she didn't even realize the
generational curse.
She gave her men everything she had instead of considering herself
first.
She was with the last man for a decade because of the years she
stuck it through.
She didn't notice her life passing her by; it's amazing what
depression can do.
She wanted to be there for him so much, her kids were being raised
on their own.

Her daughter had a baby at 14 and she got pregnant while her mom was at home.

My friend couldn't see it for nothing, as long as her man was happy so was she.

Her son walked around, holding his head down although he was as tall a tree.

He had all the potential in the world but my friend's focus was all lost.

She was so determined to keep a man in her life that her children paid the cost.

The situation got so bad; they ended up losing the dog, car, house-- they lost it all.

This was the lowest blow of her life but ya'll know He had to let her fall.

She enlisted in the Army and her man stayed home as she traveled way overseas.

She was taken out of that situation just to open her eyes to see.

She realized she had low self-esteem, weight gain, and her kids were out of hand.

How dare she go to war to take care of her family, when at home she had a man!

She looked in the mirror long and hard as she slowly fell to her knees.

Tears dropped from her eyes as she cried, "Jesus help me to start loving me!"

Sometimes God has to send you away because your life is so consumed.

He'll dry your tears and erase your fears because you are pruned to bloom!

SECOND SEED- AVOID SELFISHNESS

My next friend was so selfish, I mean, everything was all about her.

She looked down and around at everybody else when bad things would occur.

She never opened her hand for anyone, if she wasn't getting anything back.

147

She didn't hold her tongue either, nor understood the definition of tact.

She had to be seen by the "in crowd" because to her image was everything.

She didn't know why the guys would treat her bad and not consider a wedding ring.

She thought love was measured in money but nothing's free, it has to be earned.

She stuck her hand in the fire for the last time and this time she really got burned.

She thought she could trick the system by getting a handsome boy who lacked.

She figured if she clothed and fed him, he'd give her the shirt off his back.

Well, this Mr. Nobody with nothing turned out to be the worst one of them all.

He put her on a pedestal at first but soon like the rest, he let her fall.

He was incapable of appreciating a good thing because it couldn't recognize itself.

So God had to put his blinders on until she could to see it for herself.

You can only get so much from people until you eventually run out of room.

God will provide and never take away that's why you are pruned to bloom!

THIRD SEED- PRACTICE FORGIVENESS

Now, my third friend is quite a charmer, she decided to be on her own.

To conquer her fears of being hurt she opted to be alone.

Anytime someone would try to court her, she'd pull out her measuring stick.

And they were either "too this" or "too that" until no one would get picked.

She went through too much pain in her past so she decided to push everyone away.

In fact, she was so engulfed in the bad times that her future was
just fading away.
She had so many guidelines that only the liars could get in.
But no one is perfect in this world, not you, your spouse, family or
friends.
Well, God sent two strangers to her door that she just couldn't turn
away.
She had to finally confront the spirit of fear and move herself out
of the way.
An idle mind is the devil's workshop and loneliness is where it
looms.
God will help you to trust, live, and forgive that's why you are
pruned to bloom!

FOURTH SEED- CONQUER MEANNESS

My fourth friend seemed like a princess because she was as sweet
as she could be.
But I'm sure glad we were friends because she could be very
mean.
I don't think she was this way on purpose but she had been this
way for so long.
She'd wonder what your problem was like she didn't do or say
anything wrong.
She had a striking beauty to make you think she had a man, dog,
and house.
That is up until the moment she'd decide to open her mouth.
Now there was a better side to her that only her closest friends got
to see.
But God had to break down that pretty exterior just to get to her
inner beauty.
He took those she loved, her glory, her job, and all her finances
away.
He left her with just enough to get by and time to look her self in
the face.
She didn't have anything else to cling on and was forced to look at
her attitude.

She began to question herself and ask God, "Why am I being so rude?"

See, she had built a fence around her heart that no one could get in. She didn't give anyone a chance because on herself she would depend.

Well, God had to remove the freezer inside her heart to melt down the ice.

He had to get rid of the nasty attitude for her to appreciate the nice.

He had to take the sting out of the bumble just to make her humble.

He showed her; He picks her up when she falls and catches her when she stumbles.

Your life may not be what you expect but God promised your day is coming soon.

So, smile more and laugh often because you are being pruned to bloom!

FIFTH SEED- HUMBLE PRIDE

My last friend, who is the fifth, had the most struggles of them all. And it's funny with all she'd been through that she just refused to fall.

She lost her kids to the courts and her family barely wanted to be bothered.

She married a convict, who was abusive, without a clue about being a father.

She was the good girl growing up, perfect grades, a complete family, and a college degree.

Makes you wonder how a woman who had it all could end up so empty.

Well, she wasn't happy at all, the grass was always greener on the other side.

She wanted what the rich folks had because she held her status with pride.

She couldn't afford Beverly Hills but she moved there anyway. Just like her husband, she didn't even know him long but she had to have her way.

Just countless amounts of wrong turns that she refused to reconcile.

She lived the life of Mrs. Not Do Right and stayed in constant denial.

She pointed her finger at everybody for her bad husband and lost daughter and son.

Everyone was to blame for her problems and she was responsible for none.

She created all this havoc in her life that she didn't want to recognize.

Until her husband left her with child for a new woman and refused to compromise.

He did it in front of everyone, so the whole world could see.

That was the final straw; she could no longer hide- she just dropped to her knees.

There was no lie she could tell about this one, it was in the plain of day.

God had to end this mask of phoniness and put her on her face.

If she wanted things to be good, she needed God to put it all back together.

She had to learn status or possessions aren't what make families last forever.

She had to be ripped of all these false securities.

God says, "You have to die in the flesh in order to be closer to me."

My last friend died in the sunlight, at night she was buried under the moon.

By morning she grew into a precious flower and like you she was pruned to bloom!

MY FLOWER- BUILD A RELATIONSHIP WITH GOD

Now, you may be wondering, who am I to talk about my friends to such degree?

Well, I can identify with each blooming bud because they could have easily been me.

I had to learn to love myself when no one else would.

I had to learn to smile past the pain, even when it didn't feel so good.

I had to learn to give without expecting to receive in return.

I had to learn to forgive others and myself no matter how many times I was burned.
I had to learn my limitations and not succumb to pride.
I had to learn to depend on God, trust Jesus, and allow Him to come inside.
I had to be stripped down and buried deep to the point that I couldn't get up.
I had to learn to give it all to God and that's when He filled my cup!
I'm overflowing with such happiness because like some of you I didn't believe-
God would take the time to stretch out his hand and save someone like me.
When man wouldn't give me a chance and sat back waiting for me to fall-
God picked my head up, pushed my shoulders back, and helped me to stand tall.
I toiled through the darkness of the soil and was pricked by every thorn-
But I tell you when I reached the surface the most magnificent rose was born.
I thirsted but I tell you no earthly liquid could satisfy me.
Then God filled me with His living waters to help me see and breath.
And my stomach was roaring because I hungered for more to eat.
So, God blessed me with His good word, which filled my spirit with meat.
I thought I had everything until I was stripped of it all.
I had to hit rock bottom before I decided to make that call.
I looked up from the dirt of the earth and began to rise above my doom.
God raised me out of my darkness to testify that I was pruned to bloom!

We Are Beautiful Flowers Waiting to Bloom

This poem is about several women who are dealing with separate issues with a common conclusion, self-realization, and love. It's seems easy for us to look at each other and pick out strengths and weaknesses. However, it is very difficult to accept that we have faults within ourselves. I could easily identify with each flower in this poem because of my own issues that I had to deal with.

We don't see ourselves falling into these traps until we honestly reflect on our lives. I stayed in a relationship with someone that took me out of character and almost damaged the relationship between my daughter and I.

I dealt with a young man, who I knew was beneath me but he made me feel good about myself for some odd reason. Around him, I felt risky, strong, and in the end, stupid. He ended up making me question who I was and even if I was good enough for him.

I also had a point in my life where I felt it was all about my emotions, and I didn't take anyone else's feelings into consideration. As a result, I treated some people harshly because I was upset and tired of being misused.

I even chose to let some good people slip through my fingers because I was afraid of being hurt.

We are human and we all make mistakes. However, the key is not letting those mistakes get the best of us and turn us into the very monster that we are running from. We have to love ourselves enough to know that we too are beautiful flowers inside waiting to bloom.

Lip Smackin' Salmon Patties

1 can of salmon
1 egg
½ cups of fish seasoning
1/3 cup of yellow cornmeal
1 tablespoon of Worchester sauce
1 tablespoon of lemon juice
½ cup chopped green peppers
½ cup chopped green onions
½ cup cooking oil
Seasonings: salt and pepper
Frying pan
Medium bowl
Cup
Plate

1. Heat oil in pan over medium flame
2. Drain salmon juice into a cup
3. Mix salmon, egg, chopped vegetables, lemon juice, and Worchester sauce
4. Add salmon juice as need (salmon mixture shouldn't be too dry or too moist)
5. Mix pepper, fish seasonings, and cornmeal into salmon
6. Make small to medium sized patties from salmon mixture
7. Pat both sides of patty with corn meal mixture
8. Place in pan and fry until brown on both sides
9. Place on side of white rice

*Serve with wheat bread, grits, small salad or eggs

Servings: 4
Prep & Cook time: 30 minutes

Suggested Scriptures
Romans 2: 1-5,11 and 3:22-23
Philippians 2:1-3 Selfishness
Proverbs 8:13, 16:18-19 Pride
Proverbs 29:23, Matthew 5:3 Low-Self Esteem
Ephesians 4:31 Bitterness
Ephesians 4:32 Forgiveness
1 Corinthians 13:5 Love
John 6:35-39, 15:1-8

Dear Lord,

Please forgive me for every sin that I have committed. I repent and beg you to restore love and righteousness to my heart. Lord, forgive me for the sins that I did not even know I was doing against your perfect love. There have been times when I thought that I was doing everything right and pointed my fingers at others, ignoring your words of removing the splint from my own eye. Forgive me for the moments when I thought only of myself and may have neglected those in need. Forgive me for being too stubborn to say I am sorry or feeling too mighty to humble myself. Forgive me for complaining about what I don't have or how I look when there are others in this world worse off than me. Forgive me for harboring ill feelings toward others and not allowing myself to forgive them as I am asking of you. Lord, bless me with a heart of love and compassion. Although others may commit sins against me, it is not my place to be hateful or seek vengeance because you are my mighty warrior. Lord, I know I am not even deserving of your perfect love yet you keep me protected and overflowing with blessings. I just want to thank you and draw closer to you, never leaving your light and love. Help me to get over my past and forgive myself so that I can bloom into the beautiful flower you want me to be. Lord, I pray and thank you in the matchless name of Jesus Christ, Amen.

About the 19th Piece
Your Reflection

When you are single, it is hard for you to comprehend when a couple says, "I just knew he or she was the one." It leaves you wondering how they knew, what did that feel like, or did God whisper it in their ear? I am not sure of any particular right answer, except it just feels right. Not only does it have to feel right but it involves trust, as well. You'll have to seek God's guidance and not your own understanding.

Your Reflection

They say when you marry someone they are supposed to be your
reflection
A mirror of who you are or even a looking glass of where you'd
like to be
If you were happy that person would smile a lot
If you were compassionate that person would be gentle
If you were stern that person would be serious
If you were bold that person would be confident

That relationship would be like a bottomless well with waters
flowing into it constantly
You would never thirst from lack of or crave a sudden urge
Your reflection would replenish any impossibility, doubt, hunger
or curiosity

When you love someone who is a reflection of yourself,
You treat them as yourself
You would never leave yourself hungry, penniless, hopeless, sad or
shameful
You would watch your tongue and guard your ears and calm your
pride
You would shield your eyes and feed your mind and bless your
heart
You would be patient and understanding and submissive
You would be kind and gentle and oh so sweet

You would want your reflection to smile back at you with beauty
and grace
You would want your reflection to be your perfect mate

If she is sad, ask why she is crying
If she pouts, see why she is sighing
If she needs, give her what she wants
If she doubts, don't fill her with more don'ts

Treat your reflection like you would want the world to see

Isn't she just lovely?
That is because she is a true reflection of me.

A Mirror Doesn't Copy It Reflects

Finding a person that is the mirror image of yourself seems to be an exciting adventure. You feel like they may be your soul mate because you are both "so much alike". Then you find yourself feeling a bit irritated because they seem to be hogging your space. Soon that relationship becomes an annoyance and you learn that you cannot either stand yourself or there is no growth.

A mirror is not just about a copy. It is about a reflection that you can either improve upon or enhance. When you look into it you should see the truth. It is not about finding someone just like you because there is no growth there. It is about finding someone who brings out the best in you. That person becomes your reflection, the image you want to see staring back at you.

The right person has your best interest at heart even though they may say and do things you do not always feel comfortable with. It is only to make you better. Growing and stretching never makes anyone feel more comfortable. The right person pushes you and stands behind you. They encourage you and treat you how you deserve to be treated. When you look at them you should see yourself or what you aspire to be.

But, it also has to be a two way street. This means the feeling has to be mutual. You cannot just put money into a bank and not be able to get anything out of it. You have to make that person feel just as good and add to them in some type of way, as well. It shouldn't be a dependent relationship but an independent one, where you can operate alone if necessary although you both work awesomely together.

City-Fried Tilapia

4 pieces tilapia
½ cup of olive oil
1 egg
1 cup of cornmeal
Seasonings: cayenne pepper, salt, pepper, seasoning salt, garlic pepper, onion powder
Medium sized bowl
Big plate

1. Heat oil in large frying pan
2. Crack egg into bowl and add generous amounts of each seasoning
3. Wash thawed fish and place in egg mixture
4. Place cornmeal in plate and coat each piece in it
5. Fry fish until golden on both sides (about 7 minutes each side)

*Serve over green salad

Servings: 4
Prep & Cook time: 20 minutes

<u>Suggested Scriptures</u>
2 Corinthians 3:18
Ecclesiastics 9:9
Genesis 24:67
Proverbs 18:22
Ephesians 5:33
Proverbs 12:4
1 Peter 3:7
Song of Songs 2:1-3,15-16
Matthew 6:33, 10:37-39

Dear Lord,

I pray that I am a walking, talking, and active reflection of you, Lord. That people can look at me and see that I am a witness within your Kingdom walls. That they will look at me and say, she belongs to the Lord. Even in my struggles and low times I will hold my head up for the victory that is promised to me, Almighty God. I pray that when people see me, they see a reflection of my wonderful husband, Lord. I pray that I am an outstanding representation of him. I pray that they are looking into the face of a woman who is loved, in love, and has the fear of the Lord inside her. I pray that when my children see us together, they call us blessed; and when people see our children they know they are well taken care of and in good hands. Lord, thank you for showing my family the path to righteousness. Help us to keep pressing towards the mark and not be distracted by the things of this world. Bless my mate and I with an undying love and admiration for each other, so that when we leave this earth we will have a lasting impression for our generations to follow. Lord, I pray in total adoration of you and give you all the praise and glory, in Jesus' name. Amen.

Meochia Nochi Thompson

About the 20th Piece
Taking It To the Streets

When you know better you do better. It becomes your responsibility to spread the word to others and not turn a blind eye. Too many people are hypocrites; they say one thing and then do another. This type of behavior causes others to stumble and turn away from God. Also, when you keep your mouth shut and eyes closed to horrible things going on around you, you suffer guilt, as well. So, keep the blame off of yourself; just open your mouth and live by the truth that you speak! Others will benefit from your honesty.

Take It To the Streets

They will hear the trumpet sound and know the Lord is in their
mist
Many will try to call on Him but their names will not be on His list

So, run out to the streets and alleys and tell them the Lord is giving
life for free
Tell them that time is of the essence so they must cling to their
faith and believe

The man said, "Bring the poor, blind, crippled, and lame," so that
they may feast
But many were looking around at the other saying neither of them
are me

When the Lord is calling, it is foolish for anyone not to listen or
take heed
You would have to be blind, poor, crippled or lame if you cannot
see:

When your life is falling apart and you have run out of people to
blame
You may have two feet and two hands but you're not whole
therefore you are a Lame

When you've tried all you can but can't get it right and life doesn't
seem so simple
You cannot afford to lean on anyone else any more, which makes
you a Cripple

If you see what I'm saying but don't like what I say for fear of
leaving your "life" behind
Then you are visibly placing yourself before Jesus, which makes
you biblically Blind
When you have so many riches that nothing worth having seems to
affect you anymore

Your soul is still yearning for Jesus, who can't be bought, making you Spiritually Poor

This message goes beyond the pulpit
Into the heart, ears, eyes, mind, and feet
This message speaks louder than any mouth opened
And it's bigger than the dreams of the sleep
This message has surpassed every battle
And is too victorious for defeat
This message is an invitation from the Lord
So, we must take it to the streets

We must invite the poor, blind, lame, and crippled so that they can all be healed
They need to bare witness to the miraculous power of God and know that He is real

I will Repeat, the Lord is giving Life to all who will take it and the cost is free
Because when He opens His book of Life I want Him to see me!

Don't Be So Blind You Can't See the Truth

Have you ever met someone who lived in complete denial? They buy clothes that are too small. They spend more money than they have. They refuse to accept anything that is contrary to their own belief system. When someone calls them out on their ignorance the first thing they yell is: "They not talking about me!" That is what this poem is all about; people with serious issues that don't want to accept that they have problems. They don't want help and are too proud to ask for it when it is available to them.

People would like to believe that you have to be in the church to go to church but the bible says, "Where two or more are gathered, I am in their mist." It is time that we start speaking the word of truth to each other, holding each other accountable, and taking responsibility for our actions. We have to learn how to give our friends advice based off of biblical principals so they can start seeking God in their times of need. Too many of us refuse to see, hear, or speak about our problems and concerns because we don't want to hear that "church stuff". Well, reality is that people are afraid of hearing the truth because it holds them accountable.

When we sweep things under the rug, we are only allowing ignorance to flow into another generation. Open your eyes, open your mouth, and open your mind. The only way to get into a closed door is to open it. That is why God takes the lowest of low and places them high. They don't ask for anything in return. When they give, they are really giving all they have. Notice when the King, in the bible, invited his so-called friends to feast with him they didn't even want to come. But when he invited the poor they were grateful and delighted at such an honor.

I can remember my grandfather and his drinking buddies sitting outside in the alley when I was little. They would sit there talking and laughing most of the afternoon until the evening. For hours, they'd sit drinking Vodka and orange juice, beer, gin or brown liquor.

I think my grandfather's buddies inspired him to create the first speed bumps I had ever seen. He had so many grandchildren, he was afraid of someone drinking and speeding down that road and hitting one of us. So, one day he got one of those tar trucks and a ton of tiny rocks to lay down these big bumps. He created several of them down the length of the whole block. My grandparent's house may have been small but there was a lot of land surrounding it.

Anyway, Mudaddy's friends would come around everyday with their liquor, cigars, and chewing tobacco just to have a good time. But after my granddaddy had his first stroke and decided to slow down on the liquor, his friends began to scatter. After his second devastating stroke, which left him speechless, they slowed down so much we rarely saw them. These people whom he considered close friends, weren't being friendly at all.

That is how the rich people were in the story Jesus was telling about the King and his feast. They took the King for granted and were only concerned with him when it was of interest to them. The King took heed and decided to invite the people who would appreciate what others took for granted. It's the same way with the kingdom of God. If you don't accept his invitation, someone will take your place. Hopefully, it won't be a rock.

Spinach Caesar Salad

3 eggs
1 16-ounce package of spinach
1 large diced tomato
1 head of romaine Lettuce
½ package of real bacon-bits
½ cup of Caesar dressing preferred or salad dressing
1/3 cup of parmesan cheese
½ cup of shredded sharp cheese
½ small purple onion
1 tablespoon of minced garlic
½ package of garlic Caesar croutons
Seasonings: salt, pepper

1. Chop spinach and romaine lettuce to desired size
2. Boil and chop eggs into salad
3. Add seasonings, bacon bits, salad dressing, Caesar dressing, cheese, chopped onion, and diced tomato
4. Sprinkle with Parmesan cheese
5. Add croutons
6. Mix well and serve

Servings: 4-6
Prep & Cook time: 20 minutes

Suggested Scriptures
Matthew 14:12-23
Matthew 7:24-25
Matthew 11:4-6
1 Thessalonians 4:14-18
Revelations 21:12-15

Dear Lord,

Thank you for your word. Thank you for your grace. Thank you for your life and thank you for your message. Lord, thank you for allowing my blind eyes to see, my crippled heart to heal, my lame body to stand up against sin, and my poor soul to benefit from the riches of your Kingdom. Thank you for allowing me to be a witness to your good deeds and a messenger of your word. Thank you for helping me to lead by example, learn by wisdom, and experience your wonderful faithfulness. Bless you Lord, bless your heavenly name, Almighty God. This I pray in Jesus' name. Amen.

About the 21st Piece
She's A Treasure

Have you ever did something so bad that you felt God wouldn't forgive you and you couldn't forgive yourself? Maybe you got caught up in drugs or gambling, or you had an abortion, or served time in prison for a crime you committed? Back in the old days when a woman had sex before marriage she shamed her family and she could be stoned to death. Thank God that type of punishment doesn't occur today in American culture. We'd probably run out of rocks. But also, sin isn't as transparent as it was in the past. Nowadays, good and evil just seem to blend together. And, nobody wants to hold anyone accountable because they fear being considered "judgmental". No matter how we try to fool ourselves, we know and God knows sin is what it is. And it still exists. That is the great thing about the Almighty, not only does he forgive us for our sins when we confess but he wipes our slates clean. People may want to bring up your past and deliver you back into your old life but with God everything is anew. Love yourself, forgive yourself, and live your life. The victory is yours!

She's A Treasure

She doesn't know that she's a treasure
A blessing by every measure
She sees herself through other's eyes
Their truths will be her demise
She gives herself for their pleasure
Never selfish to their needs
Her body begs for some attention
And she gets filled up off their greed

She doesn't know that she's a treasure
Because no one ever told her so
She tried to quit but it ain't working
She feels there's no where else to go
The drugs stop working to numb the pain
Her heart is hurting and won't stop
She found out she can't have a baby
Now, her self is all she's got

She doesn't know that she's a treasure
She bowed her head and cried and prayed
They told her God loves all his children
And He'd wipe her tears away
She went before Him exposed and naked
Her tears spilled out upon the floor
He filled her body with his spirit
And her life awoke so rich and pure
Now she's a treasure overflowing
She has the light in her eyes
She knows exactly where she's going
And God filled her belly with life.

You Are A Priceless Treasure!

Have you ever noticed how the price of gold and silver can go up or down depending on the economy? Could it be the same way with us? Does our value go up or down depending on how we feel about ourselves? Well, in the eyes of the Lord, we are priceless.

I remember a point in my life where I did so much dirt I thought I fell out of grace with God. In my heart I wanted to dig out of my grave but I felt I was in way too deep. I just started burying myself even further; I felt like I reached a point of no return. I almost started feeling worthless. And, for a second, I began to doubt my own self and insecurity was slowly setting in. Finally, I stopped and I started asking myself why I was listening to man instead of listening to God? I began to remember that God gave me life; he brought me here and breathed life into me. It was like God was whispering in my ear and telling me to come home.

How can you measure your self worth by a sinner's eyes? You will never be perfect, if that is the case. You have to believe that you are valuable. Jesus gave his life for you. How many people will do that- give their life to a stranger? I mean, who would honestly do that? At some point in your life you have to accept responsibility for your own actions. You have to come to terms with what you have done, face the consequences, forgive yourself, and others, and move on.

Living each day to the fullest is what life is all about; you cannot do that if you are beating yourself up about yesterday. You are a treasure, a priceless treasure! It is not for anyone else to tell you that. It is like faith without seeing; you have to know it in your heart. So treat yourself like the valuable gift that you are.

Meochia Nochi Thompson

Garbage Dump Salad

4 eggs
1 lettuce chopped
1 package of spinach
1 cup of diced tomatoes
1 cup of chopped mushrooms
1 cup of shredded carrots
½ chopped purple onion
1 cup of shredded cheddar cheese
1 cup of chopped green bell peppers
1 cup of chopped red bell peppers
1 cup of chopped orange bell peppers
1 cup of chopped yellow bell peppers
1 cup of chopped cucumbers
½ cup of sliced green and black olives (optional)
½ cup of sliced banana peppers (optional)
½ cup of real bacon bits (optional)
1 cup of Italian or ranch dressing
Seasonings: salt, pepper, garlic powder
Large bowl

1. Mix ingredients together in a large bowl with desired dressing

Servings: 4-6
Prep & Cook time: 15 minutes

<u>Suggested Scriptures</u>
James 5:13-16
Matthew 7:7-8, 11:28-30
Psalm 21, 23, 32, 139:14

Dear Lord,

Invest in me Almighty God. Help me because I have fallen so many times. Give me the strength to get back up and get into the game. Deliver me and redeem me like you helped the Israelites redeem the young concubine of the Levite who was broken and destroyed at the hands of the evil Benjamites, oh Lord. I know I have sinned but I seek repentance. I want to be cleansed and cleared of my past so that I can move forward in a new life with you. I know that I am a treasure in your eyes. I know that you can see the good that is in my heart. I have been a victim for so long and I am just tired of fighting a losing battle. Keep me on your side Lord, where I am victorious and strong. Lord, release me from the bad people, bad memories, and bad habits of my past so that I can walk boldly into my new future. You said that you would go after your stray sheep. Well, thanks because I was lost and now I am found. Keep me Lord, keep my friends and family that seek your face and want to change, as well. Keep your doors open to all who come thirsting for your love. I am hungry for you and I am starving for your treasure, Lord. Thank you for seeing my value and cherishing me as one of your own. I pray with the deepest amount of love and respect in Jesus' name, Hallelujah! Amen.

About the 22nd Piece
I Want To Be That

When you find someone who treats you good and makes you feel wonderful, naturally, you'll want to make him feel the same. You like being pleased and want to please them even more to get that feeling back. Well, isn't that how we want God to treat us, with limitless love? He is yearning for a relationship with us and waiting for an invitation to bless us with life to the full.

I Want To Be That

Do you find it sweet that I love you?
And that I want to be that...your peace?
I want to be the calming sound of water to your ears
The lovely smell of roses to your nose
And the sweetness of honey to your taste
I want to be that smooth feeling of silk to your touch
And that warmth of sunshine upon your cheeks
I want to be all that is good and appealing to you
I want you to be in love with me, forever
I am your love, the one you have been praying about and claiming
for years
And you are finally here
I'm glad you haven't forgotten my words because you've been
waiting for so long
My spirit spotted you long before your flesh knew what it was
seeking
I've loved you since before time
Just believe it
Visualize and wait for my love
I will give you things so much more lasting than materialistic
possessions
You'll find that my treasures exist eternally to eternity with
goodness and faith
I accept your invitation because your heart is good to me
Now, let me be that for you, what I have been all along!
Your faithful love.

Make God the Love of Your Life

When I first wrote this poem, it was a dedication to my husband. He was the man that I was praying, writing, and asking for from God. However, when I studied the words again, I realized that it was actually about much more than my husband. It was about building a relationship with God. It was about Him yearning to be with us and waiting for us to accept His gift of life by offering Him an invitation into our lives.

You have to bare all of yourself to him; the good, bad, and the not so pretty. Only when you are truly honest with yourself can God begin a healing process within you. Only then will he be able to cleanse the unnecessary baggage and replenish you with the tools needed to help you receive all that your heart desires. Strive to be all that you can be and you will be blessed with more than you have ever dreamed.

I desired my husband long before we ever met. He was the canvas I had been painting and the words I was writing. It took years for me to work out the formula to what I truly wanted but it only took my submission for God to give him to me. Tell God what it is you want, pray, and steadfast. Keep your eyes focused on what is right and a bright future will be planted before your feet with everything you could've ever imagined or hoped for. He is all that you want Him to be.

A Roast to Relish

1 roast
3/4 cups of flour
½ cup of olive oil
2 green bell peppers
2 red bell peppers
2 yellow onions
2 can of string beans drained
1 can of corn drained
1 can of peas drained
1 can of carrots drained
2 chopped baking potatoes
1 cup of chopped celery
Seasonings: salt, garlic powder, pepper, onion powder
Roasting Pan
Large frying pan

1. Preheat oven to 350°
2. Heat oil in frying pan
3. Season roast and coat with flour
4. Place roast in frying pan, brown on both sides
5. Add water and flour and seasoning until thick gravy is produced
6. Place roast and dripping in roasting pan
7. Add vegetables and cover
8. Cook for 1½ hour, turn, and cook for an additional 1½ hour
9. Remove from oven and serve with rice

Servings: 4-6
Prep & Cook time: 3½ hours

<u>Suggested Scriptures</u>
Proverbs 8:35
John 10:14-15, 11:25-26,
John 14:6, 12, 21 and 23, 15:9-17

Dear Lord,

Thank you for taking up residence in my heart. I have opened myself and extended a never-ending invitation to your wonderful love. I love the way you love me, Lord. I desire to be closer to you. I am intoxicated with the wisdom of your words and the fullness of your promises. Lord, I want to spread the message of your love to other sisters and brothers who are spiritually lonely. I want them to feel what real love feels like. Thank you for choosing me. Thank you for giving me life. Thank you for your grace and mercy, Lord. Thank you for laying down your life for me. I know you will never leave me or forsake me. Thank you for being all that and more in my life. When my friends and strangers look at me, Lord, let them see that I am in forever love with you. I thank you in Jesus' name. Amen.

About the 23rd Piece
My Resting Place

When you are married, you should be able to find peace within your spouse. It should feel like you are at home no matter where you go or what's going on. Of course you will have your ups and downs but your mate should be the first person you want to run to for support. Do not tell all of your business to the world, instead, seek wise counsel, and pray for guidance. If you are single, seek God's kingdom. Don't get so caught up in the world that you forget what is important because without love, you have nothing.

My Resting Place

My resting place
Warm, cozy, soft yet strong
Nestled safely within the weight of your arms
Exactly where I belong
I have found my cooling place
Close by the lakeside
Caught deep between your glance
With eyes that cannot hide
There isn't any flamboyant clashing
Only a promising soft whisper of peace of mind
Where courtesy is given at the door
And foolish pride is left behind.

Nobody Really Wants To Be Alone

There are so many people who claim they are happy being alone. There are men who seem perfectly fine with not having a wife to help continue their bloodlines. Women who are so focused on their careers and traveling that they would give up being a wife. And they aren't interested in the "old-fashioned" idea of being submissive. These ideas are more serious and popular than we think. If everyone had the same thought pattern, it would literally lead to human extinction. The world cannot multiply if we don't reproduce. We need each other to make it.

Why are you partying all day, everyday? Why are you focusing so hard on your career? Why do you need to see the whole world before you commit? Are you that sure you are promised tomorrow? If you get ill, are you sure someone will be there to take care of you? Is your educational level going to mean anything when you reach 70 or will the wisdom you pass along mean more? Who will you share your experiences with and who will continue your legacy? These are questions people do not ask before they fall into the trap of saying they want to be by themselves.

It could also be seen as selfish but who would dare say caring about yourself is selfish? Of course you should enjoy life, pursue your education, travel, and go after the career of your dreams. But ask yourself why you are doing these things. You will discover the reason is not selfish at all. You are doing it to share with other people. Realizing that your real goal is to share your success with others; try hard not to push love away.

Get lost in your dreams, fall in love, enjoy your family, enjoy the life you create, and be happy doing what makes you happy. But never forget the lesson; we do what we do, for each other not to be alone. We give each other peace and that is why we fight each other so hard to keep it.

Fried Hoppin' Jalapeño Oysters

1 can of oysters
½ cup of cornmeal
2 jalapeño peppers
1 egg
1/3 cup of olive oil
Seasonings: salt, pepper, red pepper (optional)

1. Heat olive oil in a medium pan
2. Chop jalapeño peppers into tiny bits
3. Mix oyster juice, jalapeños, salt, and pepper, egg, and cornmeal
4. Batter should be loose, if too thick, add water to thin out
5. Mix in oysters
6. Fry oysters until brown on each side

*Serve with crackers and hot sauce or mustard.

Servings: 3-4
Prep & Cook time: 15 minutes

Suggested Scriptures
Matthew 19:4-9 and 21-30, 11:28-30
Romans 3:8
1 Peter 1:3-4

Dear Lord,

I seek peace and solace. You are my resting place. You are where I can find my peace. Lord, there is nobody else that can love me like you can. Help me to stay focused on the things that are important in life so that I won't be distracted by drama. Lord, I want success in this world but I don't want it at the expense of my soul or being alone. Thank you for the people you have put in my life that show me support and understanding. Thank you for your Holy Spirit that always comforts and guides me in the right direction. I know I don't listen all the time and try to find my own way but you always are there to put me back on track or pick me up when I fall. Lord, allow me to be a blessing for someone else whether it's my child or someone else's. Let me be able to share the wonderful gifts and opportunities you have blessed me with because I don't want to be completely alone. Thank you for being here for me, even when I was too immature to realize that your grace is sufficient in my life. I pray and thank you in Jesus' name. Amen.

Meochia Nochi Thompson

About the 24th Piece
Genesis of Light

Separation is something that keeps us all divided. It keeps the heavens from the earth, the good from the bad, the rich from the poor, and the sinner from the saved. And God didn't create it for evil, man did. Thank God for Christ Jesus because he provided us with a link. That link is activated through prayer! Not only did he give us a way out, he gave us a direct line to God's ear. And it's free. It's too bad more people aren't tapping into it before they make decisions. These lines of separation we are facing are much bigger than us and they keep the flesh and spirit in constant battle. It is called spiritual warfare and the only way we can fight and gain victory over it is with God's help.

The Jena 6, America's Genesis of Light

Jena 6 goes back to Genesis, the beginning.
Many are left wondering when did all of this madness begin?
While most are feeling hopeless like it may never be an end.
And each time we hear it, see it, and experience it,
The wounds seem to open again.
Although we were freed from it; it seems we are never free from it.
Instead of looking at the real picture; we are forced with another split.
Split by social economics, split by educational blitz,
Split by those who impose the law and the majority that benefits.
Split by more than just color; split by those who fight and those who choose to ignore.
Split by those who walk upright and those who use the back door.
Split by any and everything that takes us off the real issue.
Racism does exist in America and our justice system is being misused!
The Jena 6 issue shouldn't be a split.
It's about togetherness, about truth, and what is fair.
And those who stand for justice and those who choose to care!
Take away my color but don't take away my fight.
It's time to get off the side of race and get on the side of right.
For every law of righteousness, there seems to be a way for it to twist.
If you're lucky to get past one, there's another one to clamp your wrists.
Learn the law and get to know about the people you elect.
Prejudice public officials and lawmakers slip through cracks from neglect.
Voting is more than the President, the Alderman, and the Mayor.
It's about who makes the law, enforces it, and keeps it fair.
Too many politicians elected are surface and can't see beyond money or skin layers.
They push for their own agendas and don't really seem to care.
How can a country built on slavery even stand to point a finger against Iraq?

When prisons have become a private business produced off poor men backs.

Yeah, this is more than about color, the Jena 6 are America's roots being exposed.

The further the seeds of racism are buried; the larger the ugly "white tree" grows.

God was taken out of the schools after the colorless church was split into black and white.

This time justice should prevail so freedom can shine so beautiful and bright.

Because the people are crying to free the Jena 6!

America's Genesis of Light!

Love Is the Only Cure For Hate

Racism in America has been out of control for a very long time. Yes, the country finally elected a black president, Barack Obama, but it only seems to have glossed over how deep the wounds from the past really are. However, the people in America are changing with each new generation and that is progress. But our advancements are still too slow for how fast technology is moving. A race riot can get started over the entire country or world with just the click of a button.

Some may feel because it is not happening in their neighborhood or they are accepting of other races, this type of hate doesn't affect them. It does. It affects everyone who has to deal with the ugly side effects of racism.

Clearly, the incident that happened with the Jena 6 shouldn't be allowed to happen to any teenager. But, instead of people looking at the true issue, it turned into a distraction. No children who fight on a schoolyard should be sentenced to prison unless it is a life threatening or fatal incident. It's mind-boggling that during this incident the courts never raised the issue of why a particular tree on a modern day schoolyard was still being called a "white tree"? It's a terrible symbol and reminder of slavery and the hanging and brutal mistreatment of blacks. The tree should have been cut down long ago because of its disturbing history and significance.

Why is a poem like this in this book? It is here to bring awareness on how to raise your children in a world filled with separation. Make sure you raise your children to know their heritage and be proud of it, no matter where they are from. Teach them they are not superior or inferior to anyone. Show them how to appreciate and respect other's differences, social-economic status, cultures, and languages. Take your children to visit other places and taste other foods. These things don't require lots of money but they do cost you a change in attitude.

People are afraid of the unknown so they make up stories or try to conquer or fight against it. We need to teach future generations how to love more and hate less. We need to teach them to stay away from trouble. We need to show them how to fight correctly and according to God. You cannot just hate or hit people because you disagree with their lifestyle. Instead, you must learn to lead by example. Your job is to show love and speak the truth. If anyone is not willing to accept the truth, you can only, "wipe the dust from your feet" and keep on your way. Try leading with love and being objective in the next disagreement you encounter.

Rainbow Sausage

1 pound of Italian Sausage
1 green bell pepper
1 orange bell pepper
1 yellow bell pepper
1 red bell pepper
1 purple onion
1 tablespoon of minced garlic
1 cup of favorite tomato sauce (optional)
Seasonings: salt, pepper
Large pan
Olive Oil Spray

1. Add seasoning, chopped peppers, onions, and sausage to pan lightly sprayed with cooking oil
2. Heat until sausage is brown and vegetables are cooked
3. (Optional) Add 1 cup of tomato sauce and boil

*Serve over rice or rigatoni pasta

Servings: 4
Prep & Cook time: 30 minutes

<u>Suggested Scriptures</u>
Proverbs 31:1-9
Romans 8:35
1 John 2:9-14
Psalm 37:1-9
1 Corinthians 13:2-3
Isaiah 25:9

Dear Lord,

Thank you for giving me a link to your ear. Thank you for leaving your holy spirit to comfort me. I do not know why people are filled with so much hate and separation. Or why they do some of the evil things they do to each other. Lord, I am begging for forgiveness of their sins and asking you to keep my heart pure during these times. I get so frustrated and upset when I see all this injustice going on around me but I am glad that I can always remember that you will judge the wicked. Lord, I am praying that you come to bring peace to this world and restore it back to your original plan for it. I am praying that you soften the hearts of those who desire to do your will but don't so they can turn from their wicked ways. I am changed so I know it can happen for anybody. Bless my family, friends, enemies, and strangers so that they may know you are God and seek your face like I have. Lord, bring us together by bringing your kingdom to us. I love you and I adore you, in Jesus' name. Amen.

About the 25th Piece
Psalm for Release

We come up against a lot of things at home, work, and in the church that we just don't understand or seem to have control over. They affect our attitudes and how we see life and view other people. If they are not checked they can lead to years of heartache and repeated mistakes. We must learn to look beyond what we see in the flesh to the spiritual culprit and real issue. These things are known as spiritual strongholds and/or generational curses. Our only cure for these things is a good dose of Jesus. We must be trained with God's weapons of warfare. We cannot fight a spiritual battle with flesh alone. We must stay prayed up and knowledgeable in the word of God so we can recognize what we are really up against. Always remember the good news which is we are promised the victory!

A Psalm For Release

Freedom, Freedom!
Lord, free me from these chains that have come to imprison and
bind me
Bury me deep within Your bosom where no links can stretch to
find me

Let my melodies for solace be like warm honey to Your ears
As You sooth my bruised heart and gently brush away my fears

Silence the noise and confusion and make the drama cease
All I need is a word from You, Lord, just a word of release

Take me to the beginning where it all started so I can recognize it
when it comes again
Secure me firmly inside Your palms and help me courageously
conquer what's within

Help me break free of all these chains that have come to confine
me
So I can be free of all the strongholds that want to rob, poison, and
blind me

I said help me break free of all these chains, so I can get some
direction
Yes, help me shed all these weights so I can stand my own
reflection

Release the jealousy and the fear and the lies that I hear
Release the envy and the gossip and the filth from my mouth and
ears
Release the doubt and worry and the sickness and pain that are
holding me
Yes, release the baggage from my past and give me strength,
power, and victory

Release the men and the friends who have caused me to turn on
You
Release the grudges that I've been holding and the apologies that
are due
Release the mistakes and the bitterness that I've bottled up and put
on the shelf
Yes, release all the forgiveness I've been keeping from others and
from myself

Release every infirmity that stands between me getting closer to
You
And, release the idolatry, adultery, fornication, and every
perversion I ever knew

Replenish my spirit with kindness, respect, wisdom, and love
overflowing
Replace it with a spirit of joy and laughter and of confidence and
knowing
Release onto me fruits of the spirit and food for my soul
Lord, I know I am empty without You, so please come and make
me whole

Make me a servant of Your words
Lord, make me a captive to Your release
Make me a witness to Your existence
And, a walking testimony of Your peace

Freedom, Freedom!
I shout a mighty praise of victory
I am but a slave to the Lord
Freed from the chains of sin and granted RELEASE!

Break Free and Enjoy Life

Have you ever found yourself saying, "All the women in my family do this?" or "I get it from my momma?" Or have you noticed a pattern of divorce, violence or even alcoholism in your family and/or in yourself? Two things can happen when you are dealing with generational curses and strongholds; either you'll indulge in the behavior or you'll fight so hard against it that you may become a bit obsessive.

I think I was on both ends of the extreme. I noticed the patterns of marital abuse in my family and I was afraid to get married. I saw unfaithfulness so I tried convincing myself that I should be the bad one in the relationship to avoid being hurt. I noticed women who catered to strong men and let their children suffer. So, I became over protective of my child. If a man looked abusive or displayed certain behaviors I would drop him without any explanation.

The good news is that I steered clear of drugs and alcohol. However, I lived in fear that my family history was what it was and that I could not enjoy a good marriage without running into the same types of problems. Of course you will have issues in marriage but they do not have to be major issues, they do not have to define you and they can be solved and resolved.

When problems would arise in my relationships, I would immediately want to shut down and let go.

I later discovered that I was dealing with spiritual strongholds and generational curses, and that I could not fight them in the flesh. I needed Jesus' help!

I realized that my family never dealt with anything. Everyone would just sweep things under the rug and pretend it never happened. So I grew up wanting people to just shut-up and deal with it. Well, what I discovered is that people do talk back, they have opinions and feelings, and do have the right to express them. I had to learn to deal with it instead of run away from it.

I thought I was doing everything right to avoid problems but I kept getting the same results. I felt helpless. I was trying to love people who didn't want to love me back and I began to punish myself for it.

That was until I discovered that not only did I have to forgive others, I had to forgive myself, as well. Now, that was a true revelation for me because I could not figure out why I was constantly forgiving people and they continued to do the same thing to me over and over again. Basically, my ignorance made me a spiritual push over. But when I was released. When I learned that I could forgive others and forgive myself and I did not have to let them in again, I began to let go. I stood up for myself because I didn't have to take any more junk off of folks who took advantage of my kindness. I finally got rid of the drama!

I built a better relationship with my Mom because I learned to accept her for who she is and I prayed for her. I forgave my stepfather and learned to look at him and others with compassion. I learned not to take things personal because it was their issues and not mine. I even learned to express myself without running away in a relationship.

I became a finisher. I thank my husband and give him credit for so much because he would not let me shut down while we were dating. He told me that a relationship is like a waltz; whenever someone steps back you have to step forward. I applaud him for sticking by me and helping me to deal with my fears. He taught me how to identify my spiritual strongholds. My husband helped me to understand that the women in my family were good. They just didn't always make the best choices. I realized that I could control my choices and with prayer, I could make good ones.

When I began recognizing the generational curses in my family, I began bringing them down by spreading awareness to my siblings, cousins and aunts. It felt like we were getting some type of release. It seemed like we were at least recognizing and acknowledging the problems and patterns.

When you know something is not right, you don't have to accept it. You can do your own investigating, get to the cause of the problem, and pull it out by the roots. If you have been physically or sexually abused, talk about it, and help others. The more you lift the bandages and let the air hit the wound, the quicker it will heal. The fear is what keeps us boxed in and afraid to talk about things. We don't worship a God of fear but of love. So, we can face our enemies with confidence!

Now, I am not saying that once you discover your strongholds that problems and tests won't arise. I believe I was tried on several occasions. However, each time I fought back with love and the word, and I found myself getting stronger as a result.

Sit back and think about your life. Think about your own attitude and coping mechanisms. Ask yourself and then ask God to reveal where they come from, why do you feel this way, what do others say about you, and how you can fix these issues? Pray for release, pray for freedom, and pray to take your life back! Pray for restoration and redemption! You were not created for imprisonment; you were made to be free!

Stuck up and Stuffed Bell Peppers

4-6 large green bell peppers
1½ pound of ground turkey or beef
½ cup of rice
1 can of tomato paste
1 chopped small onion
½ cup of mozzarella cheese
½ cup of sharp cheese
Seasonings: salt, pepper

1. Preheat oven to 350°
2. Wash and pluck the tops and seeds out of green peppers
3. Mix meat, rice, tomato paste, onion, and seasonings together
4. Spoon mixture into each green pepper until ¾ full
5. Wrap each bell pepper in foil and bake for 45 minutes
6. Remove foil and top with cheese mixture
7. Bake for additional 10 minutes

*Serve while hot

Servings: 4-6
Prep & Cook time: 1 hour

Suggested Scriptures
Ephesians 6:12-18, 4:29-32
Titus 3:3-7
Romans 6:22-23
John 8:36

Dear Lord,

Give me the strength to recognize, pull down, and conquer the strongholds in my life and generational curses that have been plaguing my family. Give me the courage to talk about things no matter how much they hurt so that I can gain resolution and prevent others from stumbling. Give me the capacity to accept things and deal with them instead of running away. Give me compassion so that I can be more understanding and capable of praying for others to get the help they need from you, Lord. Help me to forgive others and myself as you have forgiven me countless times. Lord, thank you for answering my prayer for spiritual and physical restoration! Thank you for releasing me from my shackles. I only want to be your slave. Help me to continue to die in the flesh so that my spirit can live in you, Almighty God. I pray all these things in Jesus' name. Amen.

The End

About the Author

Meochia Nochi Thompson is a passionate Woman of God, wife, mother, poet, writer, and inspirational speaker. She is happily married to Minister Curtis A. Thompson, Founder & CEO of Wholistic Life Ministries, which focuses on blended family relationships, marital separation, divorce, leadership development and oneness with Christ. They share five very creative and beautiful children. She resides in Flossmoor, Illinois and attends Victory Apostolic Church of God under Pastor Andrew Singleton. She is a graduate of Columbia College in Chicago and has a BA in TV & Radio Broadcasting and Print Journalism.

Meochia has been writing poetry and children stories since the age of six. She spent ten years completing A Book of Poetry A Sister Can Eat To: Nourishment for the Mind, Body, and Soul. This book is packed with three things she contends to do best: talk, write and cook! She believes in "lifting the bandages so the wounds of life can heal". This book was written to strengthen the spiritually crippled and uplift the spiritually mature. Her goal is to help women discover their awesome strengths and abilities to create positive change in the relationships and world around them by unlocking and experiencing the many treasures of Christ!

To learn more about events, book signings,
speaking engagements, recipes, and poetry, visit:

http://www.meochianochi.com

Stay beautiful, from the inside out!

ISBN-10 0-9740777-0-4
ISBN-13 978-0-9740777-0-3